AWAKEN TO THE NEW WORLD ORDER

- David Dees

ZEN GARCIA
DECEMBER 2010

Those of this generation are slowly beginning to awaken to the insanity of the times as we move further and further down the rabbit hole of reality that includes the New World Order. Yahushuah bless those of you that have picked up this book in this critical time, willing to explore truth beyond the safe comforts of declared boundaries, brave enough to delve into what has always been considered the unknowable in search of the unknown. I am encouraged to see so many of you shaking off the fetters of blind obedience and acceptance of information which seems nothing more than propaganda, window dressing to keep people dumb-downed and ignorant of those things which are truly significant and meaningful to world. I congratulate those whom have moved beyond condemning position, before ever even attempting to investigate the plausibility of what I and others are exclaiming as what seems to be impossible truth.

By now, you have surely heard the catch phrase, truth is stranger than fiction. Those of you whom have dedicated self to discovering what the Illuminati, New World Order, and other secret societies are and have been up to, now know firsthand just how relevant that idiom is for our generation. This book contains the articles I wrote as a columnist for the Populist Party of America during the immediate years after the events of September 11th, 2001 and in scope share the progression of my personal awakening to the New World Order. Thus the title of this book.

Those that can grasp the relevancy of the information contained within the articles and illustrations of this book are in my opinion in better position to prepare for and warn others especially loved ones about the things that have been for hundreds and even thousands of years planned in advance for what is culmination of all of history. Contrary to accepted belief the New World Order as concept was not born with the founding of the Illuminati by Adam Weishaupt, May 1st, 1776. The New World Order is a spiritual concept masterminded by Lucifer whom became Satan the Adversary after being cast out of the upper heavens and banished to the lower earth. Prior attempts by Lucifer and the fallen angels to assert a planetary-wide global rule with impunity tyranny include Atlantis and the Tower of Babel during the time of Nimrod.

"If the American people
ever allow private banks
to control the issue of their
money,
first by inflation
and then by deflation,
the banks and corporations
that will grow up around
them,
will deprive the people
of their property
until their children
will wake up homeless
on the continent
their fathers conquered."

- Thomas Jefferson

Front Cover: David Dees, Masks

Awaken to the New World Order
© 2010 by Zen Garcia.
All rights reserved

No part of this book may be reproduced in any form or by any electronic or mechanical means including information storage and retrieval systems, without permission in writing from the author. The only exception is by a reviewer, who may quote short excerpts in a review.

Zen Garcia
zengarcia2010@gmail.com
Visit my website at www.FallenAngels.TV
www.blogtalkradio.com/FallenAngelsTV
Printed in the United States of America
First Printing: December 2010
Second Printing: September 2014
ISBN: 978-0-557-90073-2

Never Forget

Sensing impending doom, many realize that something is not quite right with world. As such they are questioning the preposterous insinuation of mainstream media news, and seeking alternative to the contrived format of corporate controlled media outlets. For those that continue to believe that there is nothing wrong with the current state of the world or where things are headed, you will most likely find no interest in the focus of this book. You may as well place it back on the shelf and go back to browsing for idle selections. However, if you are one that feels extreme urgency in the critical times we are now living in, please continue with your research, this book may assist you and others to see how late the hour is. There is much to do in preparation for those things coming. You have my permission to make and share pdf copies of this book with others. Praise the Most High that you have been lead to my work.

I thank those of you that are part of the truth network and community at www.fallenangels.tv. I invite those of you that are not, but are seeking fellowship with others that like yourself have awakened to the New World Order and other topics such as the Nephilim, fallen angels, giants, biblical prophecy, and lineage of Cain. If willing please join us for dialogue at the site, we would be honored to share some moments with you as we together, explore worlds unconventional, mysterious, and long ignored to rediscover what I believe to be some of the most important and relevant topics associated to ancient world mystery.

It was seven years ago that the Most High led me to awareness on the shadowy existence of the New World Order and their sinister plans to implement policies supporting depopulation, financial Armageddon, false flag terrorism, police state measures, unending war, order out of chaos, and fascist tyranny. These individuals are genetically linked to the seed of the serpent or line of Cain, and believe they are predisposed to rule the masses through the divine right of kings. They are duty bound to the 'Great Work' or 'Great Plan' which is the New World Order. Most of humanity has no idea that there is a separate and distinct bloodline upon the planet, which worships a different god and instead of being predisposed to benevolence, peace, and natural goodness, are genetically inclined towards evil, murder, and all things abominable as was the forerunner of their pedigree Cain, whom killed his half-brother Abel committing the first murder. Most do not realize that the powers that be that rule with oppressive animosity, are people intrinsically linked to Satan and the fallen angels through DNA, bloodline, and lineage, and that they are literally physical children of the devil or what Jesus Christ, Yahushuah referred to as the tares.

> He that soweth the good seed is the Son of man; The field is the world; the good seed are the children of the kingdom; but the tares are the children of the wicked one; The enemy that sowed them is the devil; the harvest is the end of the world; and the reapers are the angels. As therefore the tares are gathered and burned in the fire; so shall it be in the end of this world. The Son of man shall send forth his angels, and they shall gather out of his kingdom all things that offend, and them which do iniquity; And shall cast them into a furnace of fire: there shall be wailing and gnashing of teeth. Then shall the righteous shine forth as the sun in the kingdom of their Father. Who hath ears to hear, let him hear. – Matthew 13:37:43

The war that we see enveloping world is tied to the ancient prophesy of Genesis 3:15 which speaks about the enmity which began with the two sons born of Eve, Cain and Abel. Eve was called the mother of all living having sired both children. But Adam is not the father of all living, but only of the seed of the woman because Cain was his step son, a scion of the serpent. The continuance of Adam's line was propagated through Seth as Abel was murdered and never had chance to birth children to continue Adam's line. Abel was the first casualty in this ancient war.

> 15] And I will put enmity between thee and the woman, and between thy seed and her seed; it shall bruise thy head, and thou shalt bruise his heel. – Genesis 3:15

What had been portrayed in Genesis 3, and what happened in the garden so long ago is so very important for understanding where we are now and what had, is really going on in world. If you do not have discernment on this singular issue, one will be in quandary trying to understand the world condition past, present, and future. The knowledge presented in this book will help you as reader, to unlock why there is and has been such a prevalence of evil in the collective reality of humanity since our inception into this world.

> And he made a plan with his powers. He sent his angels to the daughters of men, that they might take some of them for themselves and raise offspring for their enjoyment. And at first they did not succeed. When they had no success, they gathered together

again and they made a plan together. They created a counterfeit spirit, who resembles the Spirit who had descended, so as to pollute the souls through it. And the angels changed themselves in their likeness into the likeness of their mates (the daughters of men), filling them with the spirit of darkness, which they had mixed for them, and with evil. They brought gold and silver and a gift and copper and iron and metal and all kinds of things. And they steered the people who had followed them into great troubles, by leading them astray with many deceptions. They (the people) became old without having enjoyment. They died, not having found truth and without knowing the God of truth. And thus the whole creation became enslaved forever, from the foundation of the world until now. – Apocryphon of John

For more information on the biblical side of the New World Order conspiracy, please refer to my 4th and previous book Lucifer – Father of Cain. This book, Awaken to the New World Order, focuses on the political side of the conspiracy citing a collection of articles I wrote while working as a columnist for the Populist Party of America during the years of 2005-2008. It was during those early journalistic years that I awoke to much of the hidden idiosyncrasies' associated with the New World Order and its occult endeavors. This work reflects the evolution of that rousing and how it was that the Most High helped me to decipher the illusion parading as reality.

After the presidential election of 2004, I realized that the electoral process, mainstream news, and most of what we consider as reality is nothing more than conjecture fabricated upon lies and backward assumptions. Reality truly is nothing more than a perspective that people share as agreement with others of like upbringing and cultural mind. Most have no idea what reality is or where to go to even begin to find it.

Most live in worlds based often on nothing more than what is truth as dictated by others. Most are too lazy or too scared to experience the world on their own terms, without the filter of others experience. I find essentially, that many have faith in realities which are garnered on half-lies taught by those that are either disinformers or just as lost as they when it comes to truth. The overseers of the matrix have been and are continuing to purposefully deceive the so called useless eaters, as they have an agenda to depopulate the planet, and preserve its wealth and abundance for themselves as elitist. And given that the New World Order has infiltrated all aspects of those organizations which were established to govern and impose authority over the masses, it has been easy for them to remain hidden and in control from the top down.

It is important for us as the masses, to realize this when seeking truth and attempting to glean it from the mix of propaganda fed the public. It is also important that one learn to detach from the pride of absolute knowing as I believe none of us has all the answers and that it will take dialogue, conversation, and discourse for us to come to such discernment when it comes to truth and what it really is.

For most it will be difficult to release those belief systems we have been raised upon as foundational truth; the inherited realities of our peers, pulpit preachers, politicians, and yes even parents. The truth about truth is that only a few really know anything about it, where to go to find it, and better yet how to implement it into life and being. Truth is part of the narrow way and only a few are blessed by the Most High to know anything about it.

The work contained within these pages also represents the visual chronicles of David Dees, a professional graphic artist that with his work, has attempted to shine the light of truth on the agenda of the New World Order; and like myself documents the evolution of his awakening to that which had always been behind the curtains veiled from public view. I would like to personally thank David for allowing me the use of his incredibly thought provoking images and graphic illustrations. I am indebted to you brother for your kindness and generosity. May the Lord continue to bless and protect you in your continued work and out-reach.

Please note that David depicts Zionism as evil entity, as it is controlled and historically has been funded by the transnational global elitist families such as the Rothschilds. David's images and my use of the Protocols of the Learned Elders of Zion, are in no way intended to be anti-Semitic, or racially prejudiced towards Israel as a people or a nation. We, in fact, have no bias towards any group based on race, religion, gender, or creed; and that the work contained herein does not denote a dislike, prejudice, or animosity towards Hebrews, Jews, or Israel, as a people and/or nation. Neither David nor I are anti-any people, we are anti-evil.

Those forces which have and still do finance the Zionist movement also financed the creation of central banks, and the installment of the Federal Reserve; which is a privately owned European Bank that loans money at interest to the United States which then tenders it out to the American people. This system once in place has crippled the freedom of this country and has indebted all of its citizens under its system of tyranny, enslaving us to this day. The power behind the Federal Reserve are the very same interests which own and print the money to every nation and people world-wide. They are the very same schemers which control Britain, America, Israel as well as China, Russia, and all the Muslim nations world-wide. These powerful interests are those who say they are Jews but are not but are the synagogue of Satan.

> I know thy works, and tribulation, and poverty, (but thou art rich) and I know the blasphemy of them which say they are Jews, and are not, but are the synagogue of Satan.
>
> Behold, I will make them of the synagogue of Satan, which say they are Jews, and are not, but do lie; behold, I will make them to come and worship before thy feet, and to know that I have loved thee. – Revelation 2:9, 3:9

Satan has always utilized all people, creeds, genders, and nations when fooling the masses. He utilizes controlled opposition and the creation of minorities in order to incite endless war. His agenda props up the governments which create the terrorist boogey men, installing the dictators, and breeding the criminals which later are used as justification for war, profit, and the wholesale slaughter of peoples. This is the truth that he does not want you to know. I pray there's time yet for you to awaken and understand the lateness of the hour.

Zen Garcia
10-14-2010

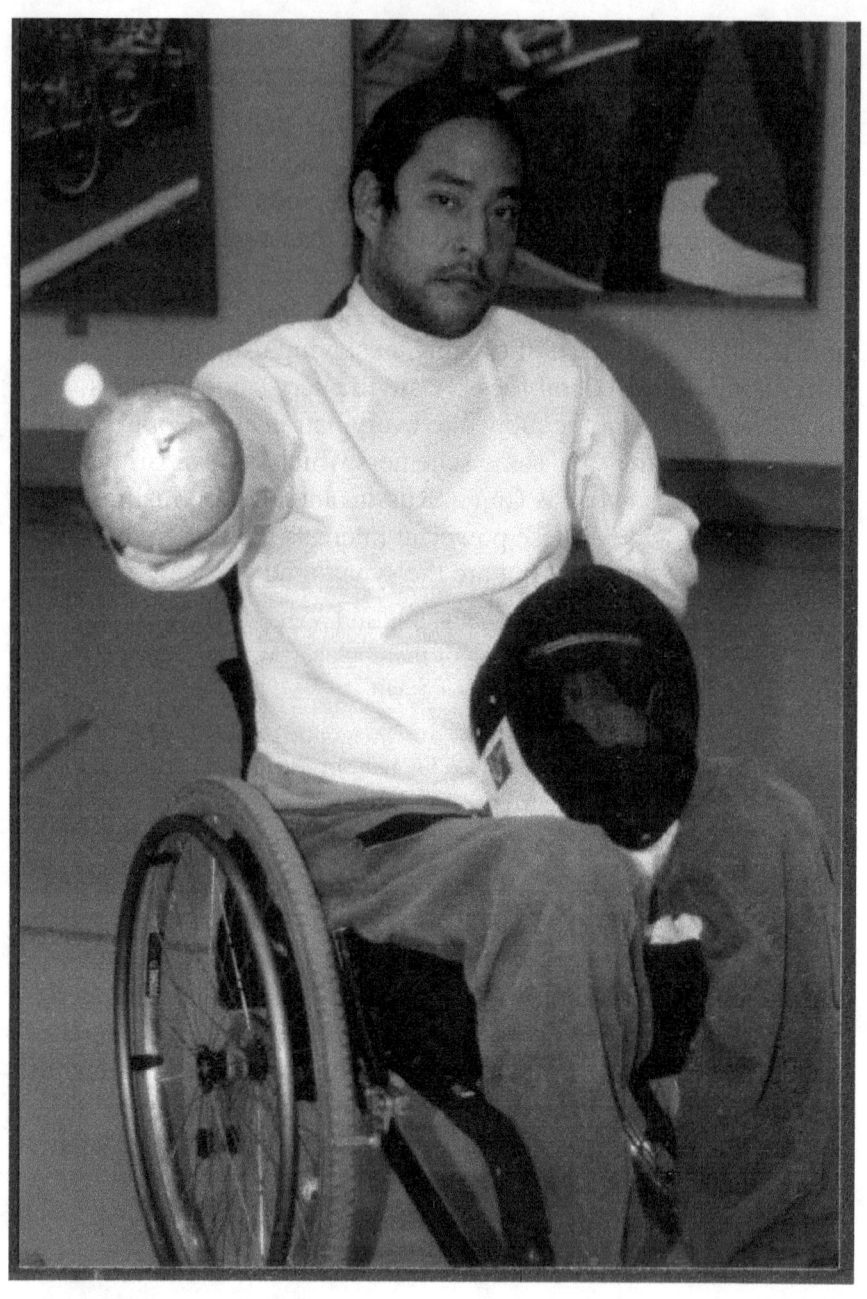

Index

The Boogey-man Disclosure - 13

Rise up Sons of Morning – 17

Tinfoil Truth - 20

Overwhelming Evidence Suggests Government Complicity on 911 - 22

The Coming Change - 27

Downing Street Memo - 29

Time to Impeach and Hold Accountable - 24

Live 8 - 35

Harsh Assessment - 39

London Bombs - 41

Peace on Earth - 37

Awake Shake Dreams From Your Hair - 47

Record Defense Budget, Tax Cuts for the Wealthy Could = Death for Many Americans Dependent on Medicaid Medicare - 49

Liar President Places America at Risk Again - 56

Support Our Troops - Tell Them the Truth - 63

The Ghosts of 9/11 - 67

The Torture King and Loss of Habeas Corpus - 73

The Lies Which Lead To War - 81

The Torture King: Target America - 88

Kissing Cousins, Staged Elections, and The False Left-Right Paradigm – 95

The Decider's Plan to Provoke War with Iran - 102

Fallen Heroes: The Return to Civilian Disability - 108

Forgotten Heroes: How many are truly injured? - 114

Giuliani vs. the Firefighters: September Criminal or 9/11 Hero? - 117

The Trumpet Sounds: People of the World Unite – 126
Can Cindy Sheehan save America? - 129
What's It Going to Take America? - 134
Open Martial Law Coming to America - 139
Domestic Spying and the Banning of Dissent - 144
Why did John Kerry Concede So Quickly in 2004? - 149
Jenny McCarty vs. the CDC - 156
An Appeal to Our Active Duty Soldiers - 164
Media Matters: Fake News and Distorted Truths - 170
Strait of Hormuz - Gulf of Tonkin Revisited - 176
The False Left Right Paradigm Continues… - 182
Where are the New Revolutionaries? 188
The Betrayal That Lead To The War of Terror - 192
Subterfuge for Larger Attack on Iran? - 197
Remembering the Fallen of 9-11 - 201

-David Dees

The Boogey-man Disclosure
Zen Garcia
December 9, 2004

The Globalists are on the run trying to cover up the loose ends which when followed concerning the events of September 11th,

2001, lead right back to the halls of an unelected shadow Government, and a certain little monkey on a string, the decider, puppet George W. Bush. I can't blame people for walking through life totally oblivious to what is truly happening around us and to us as a collective world. It's only been recent that I myself woke up to the esoteric nature of reality and 'Oz' behind the mask. As human beings, we are certainly not taught about the nature of the matrix and even after decades here upon the planet, have little if any understanding as to what this is really going on behind the scenes. What's life really all about, how did it get to this, and where are we really headed as world?

The overseers have us believing that in order to get along, we must choose path, learn a craft, and then like good little worker bees slave for the hive, and bow before the idol of materialism, strive to achieve abundance, and with our wealth support the macro-economic scheme of government, industry, production until reaching the golden promise of retirement at age 65. Of course most never make it, social security itself a legal Ponzi scheme.

At least the world is waking up somewhat I can sense urgency in the attitude of disgust and criticism enveloping mood of people as the New World Order openly declares its mandates, tightening vice like grip on the throats of the masses. At least some of the once proud American people, realizing their subjugation, are shaking of the fetters of sad transformation. Some are yelling patriotic anthems to stir the pathetic docile spit dribbling masses glued to imbecile TV. Rebels around the world are sounding trumpet as most of the world citizenry continues in pattern and routine of nonchalance, disregarding the outcomes, circumstances, and effects of American foreign policy and its ill affects upon the world.

Political leaders everywhere rise in contempt knowing something must give. Doom foreboding, many realize that governments across the world establish, fund, and train terrorists if only to ensure continual and increased funding for security and police state measures. The powers that be and I will name them through-out this work are using terrorism as a way to push an agenda of perpetual war, profiting from both sides.

They have duped America into supporting a patriotic charade wherein they can at any-time have the boogeyman, the invisible jack in the box spring out unawares to terrorize the masses at the most convenient time. This revelation is no easy knowledge; even I too was tricked for longest time and when confronted with such discernment continued to deny the truth of it. Nobody wants to admit that we've had the wool pulled over our eyes for so long.

Scoffers and deniers will become hostile to anyone who challenges the accepted belief system of those who think they know what's going on. Many claim expertise parroting the bobble-heads on TV paid to sway public opinion, being indoctrinated into such assumption from the safe and secure comfort of their living rooms. They assert the perspective of the same media pundits pranced out as terrorism experts, whom bold faced lied when speaking about, or sharing commentary upon the actual events of September 11th, 2001. Those not selling the war were quickly canned as the events of that day were used by these same so called experts to manipulate the American people into determination for war against the innocent nations, peoples, and children of Iraq and Afghanistan. The controlled manipulation of the 9/11 events were utilized by political representatives as catalyst for a war on terror which Dick Cheney proudly declared would not end in our lifetimes and now both parties are lined up ready to tow the line in supporting dubya for invasion especially since the public has bought into the official lie connecting Al-Qaeda to Iraq, when even Al-Qaeda was not responsible for the 9/11 attacks.

It's clobbering time even though most Americans do not agree with action based on contrived evidence, in support of illegal, immoral, and unjustifiable war. And not only war but extra-ordinary rendition, torture, the use of depleted uranium, destruction of families, children, lives, and infrastructure, all collateral damage as the war machine gears up for slaughter and massacre minds cannot fathom. Hopefully soon the world citizenry will awaken to and accept that yes parts of governmental hierarchy were, are, and had been responsible for not just the false flag events of September 11th, 2001, but many such events used as reason to incite war or aggression against patriots, peoples, groups, and nations such as the earlier WTC attacks September 11th, 1993, the Oklahoma City

Bombing, Waco tragedy, Gulf of Tonkin incident, and yes even the successful Japanese attack on the morning of December 7th, 1943, the day of infamy. When people learn how governments sponsor terror in order to assert agendas, it will be like the sun rising, inching slowly over horizon to disperse night in quick revelation.

> The real menace of our republic is this invisible government which like a giant octopus sprawls its slimy length over city, state, and nation ... It seizes in its long and powerful tentacles our executive officers, our legislative bodies, our schools, our courts, our newspapers, and every agency created for the public protection ... To depart from mere generalizations, let me say that at the head of this octopus are the Rockefeller-Standard Oil interest and a small group of powerful banking houses generally referred to as international bankers. This little coterie of powerful international bankers virtually run the United States Government for their own selfish purposes ...They practically control both parties, write political platforms, make cats-paws of party leaders, use the leading men of private organizations, and resort to every device to place in nomination for high public office only such candidates as will be amenable to the dictates of corrupt big business ... these International Bankers and Rockefeller-Standard Oil interests control the majority of newspapers and magazines in this country." – John F. Hyman, Mayor of New York City 1922

-David Dees

Rise up Sons of Morning
Zen Garcia
December 22, 2004

Four years I lived in a van, wandering the American countryside, subsisting for weeks, months at a time in the quiet serenity of the various national parks dotting the landscape of America. Age 22, I spent these introspective moments contemplating the largest questions mind could conceptualize, inspiring discourse which immortalized to poem became content for my first publication, "Look Somewhere Different." Having found voice and audience to reflect upon message, I decided to break free from the routines of normalcy, deciding instead of corporate 9-5 to embrace uncertainty, and the mystery freedom of life on the road. Like Kerouac, I would chase mythic acclaim, wonder of moment chasing elusive sun to ocean horizon where it would leave me defeated with Venus as assessment for new disposition.

This dynamic changed my life, for first time I cared about what I said and how I promoted message. I became conscious of what I was leaving behind as written legacy. Never before had I felt such connection to streams of letters scrolling across pages of description and conveyance. When I broke my neck in '94, following losing our brakes and going off a cliff in California, I found myself having to reassess, reevaluate and remold life and to pick up what was left of the unbroken in attempt to gather myself anew. That period of my life lead me to involvement with ADAPT and Not Dead Yet and the struggle for the rights of people with disabilities. For nine years I wrote for different disability magazines, establishing myself with voice in four states spread across the Southeastern United States, reaching a community connected loosely in internet-instant. New was the quick advent, access to each other's thoughts and ranting.

Life was simple then. Still blissfully ignorant and patriotic to the core, I never imagined that the world could be gripped and completely altered by the events that came to be September 11th, 2001. The incident changed me forever as I began to consume the onslaught of media stories connected to this scenario. For 3 years I studied all I could find linked to this event. The impression of which was burned upon my soul. 9/11 became the catalyst for my current quandary; deciding how to utilize this knowledge for betterment of humanity especially at a time when most still have no clue. What to do? Speak truth to power or? How can I continue my role as an advocate, poet, writer for the disability community when I carry knowledge of a larger evil than the one I confront in those roles? Do I carry this quietly within, sharing discourse with others also in the know when moment allows? And so, I wander gripped by this dilemma day after day, leaning more to that mindset that I cannot afford to sit on my hands and do nothing, that I must put aside all worry and do what any great patriot would do - put word out that we are under attack and that the real terrorists are hiding in our own government in plain sight. Who knows where to from here? But I have great hope that those that oppose war and love life will take back this country and make it great once again, a beacon of renewed hope, freedom, and equality for future generation.

"Naturally the common people don't want war; neither in Russia, nor in England, nor in America, nor in Germany. That is understood. But after all, it is the leaders of the country who determine policy, and it is always a simple matter to drag the people along, whether it is a democracy, or a fascist dictatorship, or a parliament, or a communist dictatorship. Voice or no voice, the people can always be brought to the bidding of the leaders. That is easy. All you have to do is to tell them they are being attacked, and denounce the pacifists for lack of patriotism and exposing the country to danger. It works the same in any country."

– Hermann Goering, Commander in Chief Luftwaffe, Nazi Germany

- **David Dees**

Tinfoil Truth
Zen Garcia
January 16, 2005

Listen people, it is critical that we stand for traditional American values and combat the Bush administration attempt to normalize torture, making it acceptable in the minds of our citizens as well as world. Please understand that our military and intelligence assets are literally acclimating torturing as tactic and abusing people to death in sadistic ways, and not just in rare instance, but as a matter of post 9/11 war on terror policy. We absolutely must hold our leaders accountable now or mark my words we will reap the injustice of what's going on, someday. Do you not get it that the decider met with Blair and set plans for the invasion of Iraq long before covert powers pulled off the events of 9/11? Study the Downing Street Memo and then support John Conyers and the other 89 Representatives that have signed on to his congressional query demanding President Bush explain the contents of the memo. It is essential that we learn the truth about 9/11 as it is what government cites as justification for the push for war against both Afghanistan and Iraq.

The official story cannot explain how three towers WTC 1, 2, and 7 all went down supposedly due to burning jet fuel when never has a steel structure before or since ever lost structural integrity due to fire. Also we must emphasize that only two of the three buildings which collapsed that day, had been struck by an airliner to provide reason according to the official account for the buildings implosion.

Another serious anomaly, no residual outside of the Pentagon of what would be remnants of an actual plane crash involving a massive Boeing 757 jet airliner. Try finding anything resembling actual parts of flight 77, plane, bodies, luggage, or impact trail which would bear witness or resemble such a tragedy. It's not possible even with mainstream news attestation that the DNA of every passenger had been located and verified with the remains found there.

The official story is an obvious, blatant lie and not even a good one at that. Wake up America, before it is too late. Foreign UN peacekeeping troops are already amassed on our soil protecting the very FEMA camps the shadow government wants to put you in later. Remember that the elites of various European countries had prior to World War II funded and put into place the infrastructure that later was utilized by Hitler and the NAZI SS for genocide against those targeted for destruction. If the NWO elites ever pass the law to confiscate American guns and desecrate our 2nd amendment right to bear arms, as they intend to do through United Nations resolutions; imprisonment won't be far behind for Christians, patriots, constitutionalists, and those who truly love our country. Also remember though, that it only took 5% of the American population to kick the British out of this part of the world during the Revolutionary war for our nation's independence. The British Navy and Army was at that time the most feared military force in the world. Get busy people there's much work yet to do.

"Well, Doctor, what have we got—a Republic or a Monarchy?"

"A Republic, if you can keep it." - Benjamin Franklin— close of the Constitutional Convention 1787, when queried as he left Independence Hall on the final day of deliberation.

- David Dees

**Overwhelming Evidence Suggests
Government Complicity on 911
Zen Garcia
February 18, 2005**

I did not learn the truth behind the events of September 11th, 2001 until after the 2004 election debacle, when John Kerry conceded the hopes of the world citizenry to his cousin George W. Bush. As in most elections the people are not truly represented and there is really no viable choice. Just as the anti-war movement really had no candidate to support or endorse even though they, like the rest of America, jumped on the "Anything but Bush" bandwagon, we the people are only presented with the illusion of choice and the illusion of representation in the electoral process. I at that time did not know that John Kerry and George Bush were in fact cousins, and that both had prior to their candidacy sworn allegiance to a secret society, a freemasonic organization known as the Yale death cult Skull and Bones. Then with the release of Michael Moore's Fahrenheit 9/11, I learned about the Bush family's intimate relationship to the Saudi royal family and in particular, the Bin Laden family. And while American and world citizens, were grounded by the FAA imposition banning all air travel through American airspace during what was the height of tense uncertainty following the supposed impacts of the World Trade centers and Pentagon by hijacked Boeing 757 flights, the Bin Laden family had been exempt from such ban and were allowed to exit the country unhindered when supposedly it was Osama Bin Laden that had masterminded and orchestrated the attacks of that day.

If this singular piece of evidence does not pique your interest and send up red flags as to how and why this family of all people were allowed to leave the country in such quick fashion and with the consent and approval of the president, at a time when every intelligence agency was pointing the finger at Osama, is absolutely beyond belief and completely and utterly mind blowing. This knowledge fueled my intensive research into the Bush family, Osama, and events leading to and during 9/11.

I will never forget the visual of the Twin Towers on fire, smoldering, people jumping in desperation from its magnificent height. The horror of desolation the inhabitants must have felt entrapped inside and then the stupefaction of all who were glued to televisions world-wide as the Towers were gutted in implosion, huge plumes of dust ejected in flutter as twisted steel rained down from above, concrete having been pulverized into a fine powdery mist. No one expected the towers to fold in upon themselves at break-neck speed, and why would we, buildings don't just fall in on themselves and not at free-fall speed. Every one sensed something not right with the events we just witnessed.

The fire fighters themselves reported explosion after explosion happening on all levels of all three World Trade Center buildings as suspiciously all collapsed upon themselves. Larry Silverstein reported in a PBS documentary special about 9/11 that a decision was made to 'pull the building,' industry terms for a what amounts to controlled demolition and this only months after Silverstein's conglomerate had purchased and insured heavily those buildings.

I initially like many full blooded star spangled patriotic Americans, had total confidence in a just government and the integrity of our elected leaders. I like most clamored for revenge and retaliation against those who would dare attack our nation and people. Imagine my disgust as years later my confidence obliterated, I like many others finally came to the realization that like most of the world, I had been played for a fool. Suckered into supporting exactly what the powers that be wanted all along, precedence to invade and destroy. I was literally dumb founded when initially grasping the overwhelming evidence which clearly demonstrates that a rogue element within our and other governments were and are responsible for allowing not only the military stand-down of that day but the suppression of many efforts to warn our intelligence apparatus so as to ensure the terrorist attacks of 9/11 went down successfully that day.

Before my awakening like most Americans I gave the benefit of doubt to those forces I trusted were in place to protect, preserve, and serve. Like the police I wanted to trust government and those taking part within it; to honor their duty and authority over the lives of myself, child, and what would be future American posterity. Dupe again are we not morons for assuming that we as a citizenry could trust individuals to wield power without corruption. I mean did not our forefathers warn of just such a thing?

> "That whenever any Form of Government becomes destructive of these ends, it is the Right of the People to alter or to abolish it, and to institute new Government, laying its foundation on such principles and organizing its powers in such form, as to them shall seem most likely to effect their Safety and Happiness."

> "…mankind are more disposed to suffer, while evils are sufferable, than to right themselves by abolishing the forms to which they are accustomed. But when a long train of abuses and usurpations, pursuing invariably the same Object evinces a design to reduce them under absolute Despotism, it is their right, it is their duty, to throw off such Government, and to provide new Guards for their future security."

Unwarranted trust had made us lazy, long ago the people had surrendered due diligence and became comfortably complacent. We were not a vigilant citizenry as most did not even participate in representative government when it was yet still worth the effort. Now it's too late as the old monarchy of tyrant kings has been covertly restored so that the president represented the public façade of backroom dictators.

How quickly, the military was given green light for the invasions of both Afghanistan and Iraq. Written prior the Patriot Act was forcefully enacted as legislation, murdering Constitutional rights and freedoms; passed by Senate and House without just scrutiny never even having been read. Now guilty until proven innocent, gestapo powers granted policing agencies, the new Homeland Security. 9/11 was an Illuminati coup d'état, declaration to world that the elitist secret societies and freemasonic power structure was fully in charge having wrestled control completely from legal authority. The agenda for world government, order out of chaos, and the reign of the anti-christ was in high gear. Having stolen such power they could lead the world should they wish even into the very pits of hell.

Our right to privacy has been thrown asunder, the voices of dissent punished as example to others who would dare stand for the rights or freedoms of We the people. Governments of the world had been put on notice, the criminal banksters are in charge, justice and the rule of law would benefit the robber barons. Invasions and wars would be waged for the sole purpose of securing natural resources for corporate enterprise. Political favor would be bought through kickbacks and bribes. Loans would be offered and secured by the partners of the World 'Fascist' Bank as way of financing dictators and oppressing, subjugating populations. These 'humanitarian' deals would ensure opening the world's natural resources to privatization, bankrupting countries, and strapping their economies with insurmountable debt placing them further at the mercy of wealthy nations and elitist regard.

The world is attempting to organize revolt against such tyranny. Global movements are coming together, to force changes upon the puppet governments that the globalists have established worldwide.

Their plan to merge world in unified government controlled by them through the United Nations Security Council, has faltered in setback as the French and Danish governments have voted down approval of the European Union Constitution, citing loss of national sovereignty. Americans are also protesting against the Pan-American union goal of merging Canada, the United States, Mexico, and all the countries of Central America.

Many understand now the predicament that we find ourselves in. As awakened patriots we must warn each other and wake others up as much as possible to the evil breeding across the globe. It is necessary for this time that we each share what we know, for in sharing what we know we might turn this country around.

> "The idea was that those who direct the overall conspiracy could use the differences in those two so-called ideologies [marxism/fascism/socialism v. democracy/capitalism] to enable them [the Illuminati] to divide larger and larger portions of the human race into opposing camps so that they could be armed and then brainwashed into fighting and destroying each other."
>
> Myron Fagan

- **David Dees**

The Coming Change
Zen Garcia
March 6, 2005

Out of all the people I personally know, my uncle is the only person who has any sort of understanding as to what's going on in America and the world. Of all the people he knows, I am the only person he can speak to openly about things which for the most part are little unspoken about, but in truth should have the most significance for our country and the world. Both of us are and have been truth seekers for most of our lives even though the things we were researching at the time seemed to be worlds apart. Eventually our studies lead us full circle and into each other's area of interest. Now both of us have eyes to see and ears to hear. Now we are able to piece things together for each other and fill in the gaps together which greatly enables us to grasp the full picture of what's really up.

For those of you who think you're crazy because you are starting to wake-up to the true nature of reality, and are questioning yourself as to why so much terror has taken hold of the planet; you are not alone and now many people sit right where you are. We are glad you're waking up. We need your help. We need you to learn everything you can about the New World Order, Learned Protocols of the Elders of Zion, Northwoods, Bildeberger, Council on Foreign Relations, PNAC, and the United Nations plot against the rest of the world conspiracy. The elitist want a global population reduction of 85% so that they can come out into the openly control the masses with impunity. They do not deny their plans to purge the masses into a manageable servant class. This conspiracy has been going on for centuries. One should look into Manly P. Hall's The Truth of All Things Never Told to really understand what is taking grips of our collective fate.

9/11 allowed the spread of terror to all parts of the world. At least now their plot is open to scrutiny, as the official story is a ridiculous failure when it comes to explaining the events of that day. Even though they busy themselves outsourcing terror, we are sharing with all who would listen and all who can see what's really going on.

NOT A SINGLE ANNOUNCEMENT WILL REACH THE PUBLIC WITHOUT OUR CONTROL. Even now this is already being attained by us inasmuch as all news items are received by a few agencies, in whose offices they are focused from all parts of the world. These agencies will then be already entirely ours and will give publicity only to what we dictate to them. – Protocols of the Learned Elders of Zion, 12:4

- David Dees

Downing Street Memo
Zen Garcia
May 26, 2005

Today I watched a congressional inquiry into a secret for UK intelligence eyes only report leaked first to the London Times called - the Downing Street Memo. This secret document is the minutes from a July, 2002 meeting between Bush and Blair where the case for an invasion of Iraq was found to be so weak that they would have to fix the facts to fit the agenda for war and then lie and manipulate the American people and Congress into supporting an invasion of Iraq. Clearly what they did was illegal and amounts to crimes against humanity. 560,000 American citizens joined a 125 Congressional Representatives in petitioning the White House for what many are claiming are impeachable offenses. Lead by senior congressman John Conyers, the President, Vice President, and

Secretary of Defense were all asked to speak to members of Congress about their deception for war. Why is this information important for those of gathered here today for this o so important inquiry? It is precisely because $300 billion dollars has been spent already to fund the war in Iraq and the Iraqi people are worse off now than when Saddam Hussein was in power. On Thursday 23 October 2003 Truth Out reported, "A new Iraq scandal erupted today as a report claimed billions of dollars earmarked for rebuilding the country have vanished after being handed to the United States-controlled Coalition Provisional authority." 8 billion dollars of American tax payer dollars disappeared without a trace while we the people are asked to bear the cost of the war by doing without on domestic spending.

For people with disabilities reliant on the government through the Medicaid and Medicare systems, cuts from above represent life and death for many of us deemed too costly for government assistance. I have been hit with cuts to my hours and levels of care as well as having my rental assistance decreased so that now I have to pay double what I did before. How many people would the $300 billion that we've already spent funding the war have helped here in this country if we would have used it to support the American people in issues such as long term care, general health care, and education? How many jobs could have been created, businesses began, students supported? In the times ahead Americans are going to have to be increasingly vigilant that our representatives in the White House, Congress, state, and local branches of government are well aware of our desires, wishes, and hopes; so that they do not deter from caring for the citizens of our nation. You can bet that they will continue to erode public service and welfare programs in efforts to maintain defense spending and benefits for the rich.

To the size of the state there is a limit, as there is to plants, animals and implements, for none of these retain their facility when they are too large. - Aristotle

- David Dees

Time to Impeach and Hold Accountable
Zen Garcia
May 28, 2005

It is really past time for America to wake up. The sooner people start to look into all the issues that are affecting us, THE BETTER OFF WE'LL BE. We as a population should have been on the streets of D.C., amassing in the halls of Congress, in the face of our Governor's and Representatives', declaring loudly no fricken more, you people are out of control and must be stopped at all costs. We have to force dialogue with the idiots on the hill as they implement policy and legislation which will only bankrupt our children's future hopes and dreams. We are being led into illegal wars and being opened to the terrorism the administration claims they are fighting. If we were really fighting a war on terror, would not the first thing a nation would do, be to secure its borders? It's important that those of us that are in the know not sit back and just watch our country be destroyed by the Illuminati elite and those that serve as pawns to their agenda. If you know that they are leading your family to slaughter are you not going to in the least attempt warning? We must if one has any semblance of conscience speak up. The elites plan on subduing this great nation, wrecking her so utterly that she will be on her knees begging international interests to save her. Sequestered we'll be forced to bow admittance to a one world government socialistic system taxes the collective populations of the world. We must lay the line that we know what's up, what they're up to, and that we're not going to go along just to get along but that each of us is going to empower the other to stand up for the rights and freedoms we all deserve as a collective. If you're not fighting for the future hopes and concerned for the dreams of a yet unborn generation and like one whose mindset is to ignore the things of today which lead to the problems of tomorrow, then you're part what's wrong with the country today. It's time to learn the truth and to share it loudly, to not do so would be treasonous to our country.

Keep calling and keep flooding Washington with emails, there is no denying the relevancy of the Downing Street Memo. Try as they might there is no way to squirm their way out of this. And even though they desperately want this story to disappear don't let up and don't get distracted. This memo is pivotal to spark a 9/11 movement for truth. That's why it's up to each and every one of us to keep this issue alive and force an evacuation of Iraq as soon as humanly possible. Once it is determined that this is an illegal and not just an immoral war, Congress will be forced to quit paying for it, the Iraqi and Afghani people themselves would then have knowledge to force out the illegal occupations of their countries. The faster we can end all this war on terror not to end in our lifetime's insanity, the better off the world will be when it comes to renewed spending for domestic programs. It is the only way we will ever be able to restore and take care of the people of the world the way we should be taken care of. If we let this issue die, they will have won another decisive victory against us. Please people wake up, we absolutely must hold our leaders accountable for the lies and deceptions played out on the many occasions they have duped the public into supporting not only this but so many other illegal and totally immoral wars of conquest and occupation. Up until now some 1700 US troops have died unnecessarily and tens of thousands, if not hundreds of thousands of innocent Iraqis and other Muslim nationals have been killed or tortured in the many prison black sites the Bush administration has set up all over the world. Just the fact that we know our government is torturing people in our names should bring every American pouring out onto the streets in absolute disgust and irrevocable anger. We should protest en masse every day and shut down the routine of everyday business as usual attitudes by overwhelmingly shutting down the function of government and politics of death and destruction. Do you know many innocent people have been tortured to death while in US custody?

Wake up America - this is not a government representative of the people or one that listens to the wishes of its people. This is a government that serves the corporate elite and one that bows down to the intent of the globalist bent on depopulating the planet. People don't believe me when I say that they actually have in place documents which support my position and that they are in fact not trying to hide anything but are openly boasting about how stupid the American people are as useless eaters and how unnecessary worry was in attempting to hide the truth of the agenda since we as cattle are too dumb to realize or do anything about being lead to slaughter.

They are largely succeeding at depleting large populations of human beings through depleted uranium munitions, vaccination, and secretive forced sterilization programs. I know for those that have never heard this or that like I once had totally trusts in government and the soundness of doctrine and policy put forth by those serving in an elected capacity, this sounds totally crazy the gibberish of a conspiracy theorist, or one who whose been overly medicated, a poor delusional soul conversing with ghosts or counterfeit demon. For most like myself, truth of such a capacity will be no doubt the hardest thing to face. Many will shun any information which leads to it and hide from any reality which exposes it. But the fact is truth is truth in whatever package it comes dressed in, whatever form it takes. We can ignore it or deny it, neither defines it true form.

In my opinion it better for us to face truth sooner than later. As one in the know, realize I am watching for your awakening, instructed to give you the keys to the kingdom. I will whisper to any whom would care to listen, truths so large they must not be tossed as pearls before swine as most have no respect for truth nor do they have a capacity to recognize it as something that should be honored, cherished in its capacity to set minds free. If willing I will share with you the research I've gleaned in learning about those forces aligned against us.

It does no good to beg or wish others do their research; those that are ready like us shall be driven to seek. The lost we must pray for. I believe it absolutely imperative for our children, nation, and world that we wake up the American people. The fate of the all hangs in the balance and those of us in the know, must warn others what the wealthy elite are trying to bring in as New World Order, and how this equals global serfdom under tyrannical rule. We are the front lines of the true planetary wide war on terror as the real battle is being fought moment by moment by each of us individually as we attempt to decipher truth from the constant stream of propaganda being spewed out as reasons for accepting and believing a reality which goes against common sense. I pray for all of us.

For my friends camped out in the Tennessee Governor's office for the fourteenth day, We support your every effort and stand with you in citizenship to hold accountable all these corrupt politicians bought for and sold out to the corporate powers influencing our legislation. Know that we too have confronted our Governor and were forced in to acts of civil disobedience just accomplish future meeting. This is true democracy in action. Wake up America; you are needed now to act more than ever.

"If the people knew what we had done, they would chase us down the street and lynch us." ~ George H.W. Bush to Sarah McClendon

- **David Dees**

Live 8
Zen Garcia
July 2, 2005

Saturday July 2 and I could receive no better gift than waking up to Live 8 to watch with the world a concert whereby the planet was informing the G8 leaders following the Bildeberger agenda - WE ARE WATCHING YOU. Over 20 million people came together to inform leaders of the wealthiest countries of the world, we want you to help Africa, to in the least take care of the lowest among the lowest as far as a people wracked in poverty, AIDS, and disease. That we as a world citizenry want them to work on eliminating hunger and providing clean water to all people everywhere but especially in Africa. We know they secretly don't want to help and have in fact waged war against the populace for centuries. They like their parents and grandparents are following a plan to depopulate the planet and eliminate large numbers of people from the gene pool. Look up Kissinger's Population Council and the Club of Rome and their links to depopulation for more info on this.

They are not even trying to hide their protocol. It is official policy embraced by the United Nations and all governments of the industrialized world. Those that print the money, set up the stock exchanges, own the banks, and through their enormous wealth control all governments want the useless eaters dead and the rest remaining to be servile slaves to their upper echelon right to dominate and rule. Who are they? They consists of a very small group of internationals bankers, financiers, Old money Royalty, and all leading members of industry, corporation, media - print, TV, Cable, etc called the Bildeberger Group.

They want world government and global control but they have a problem, the American people are among the most well armed group of people anywhere in the world and because they are having difficulty forcing through legislation to where they can just outright kill us, they will eventually attempt to disarm American citizens. In the meantime you can bet that they will poison populations by adding contaminants to the food, water, and air. According to the Report from Iron Mountain, they will also use other means such as abortion, the death penalty, euthanasia, vaccinations, etc to decimate the populations everywhere so that seizing control will be easier for the New World Order.

The Illuminati use governments to kill off their citizens with the ultimate con of getting public support in various countries for wars which cause more depopulation and centralize power even further for the globalist agenda. That is why immediately after WWI and WWII you had a call for the League of Nations and lastly the United Nations. Now that they have a United Nations they are using the various world UN organizations to push their agenda further through third world vaccinations, forced sterilization, etc.

The United Nations will be portrayed as a good organization, one dedicated to peace and security but what people do not realize is that the United Nations is, has been, and always will be a front group for the global elite. America will be condemned as a rogue nation with American credibility dissipating rapidly it's just a matter of time before the power of the United Nations will be preferred over American hegemony and the British/American/Israeli Empire. America's stand for morality and human rights has been destroyed purposely through the use of torture and scandals taking place everywhere in all the houses of horrors set up across the world by the C.I.A.

The global elite are planning the destruction of America by fostering the hate now being perpetrated all over the world by orchestrated massacres on civilian Muslim populations. In a one world government no one nation can be great and no one people powerful because such a nation cannot be controlled openly by the global world government. The next global war is being set up to be a 3rd crusader war between Western Christian nations against Eastern Muslim nations and their Communists supporters. The next war is about massive killing and order out of chaos. They want enough people to die that it will be easy for them to maintain control of populations. The globalists worry now because we are not at a manageable level. The fact is if everyone woke up to their agenda, we could quash them like a pack of rabid dogs.

Nations will war with nations over resources and many people will die if you people out there do not wake up and realize that yes there is a force in the world that wants war and destruction and is clearly bent on depopulation. What is also true is that force is connected to the Bildeberger group, Council on Foreign Relations, Trilateral Commission, United Nations, and Bohemian Grove agenda; all fronts for the global elite. They are identified. We know who they are. We must warn others. The only thing that scares them and threatens their very lives and agenda is an informed citizenry. A force of millions that knows their agenda cannot be fooled to go along with their plan. Not only that but a force of millions that knows what they are trying to set up through the governments of the world just because they own all the banks in the world and the media to keep the masses dumbed down- will not tolerate such people operating in the free world and that is what scares them the most.

It is a race their advancing agenda setting up the police martial law states for one world government totally and openly controlled by them and our rush to share knowledge and open minds to the existence of a few families of people wanting death and destruction on the planet. They for some reason love destruction death and profit from the wars they create. The Live 8 was a great beginning move towards an informed world citizenry. It will take more than just one day of being exposed to the power of the G8 to learn the true agenda. Take the time people, our collective lives depend on it.

Let's keep the pressure on.

> **One would think by listening to all the propaganda about the United Nations that they are some sort of benevolent, peaceful organization. Never in the history of the United Nations has it stood for anything but killing and violence. They have never kept peace anywhere on this globe. Their sole function is to replace the U.S. military - dissolve all four branches of our armed forces. Their allegiance is only to the United Nations Charter which does not recognize the U.S. Constitution. This body is made up almost exclusively of communists and leaders of the bloodiest regimes on this globe. Their history and operating agenda is apparent to anyone who takes the time to sincerely and with an open mind, research the facts of this organization, separating truth from myth. Bilderberger participants (another group committed to one-world domination) in 1992 called for 'conditioning the public to accept the idea of a U.N. army that could, by force, impose its will on the internal affairs of any nation.'** – Paul Harvey

- **David Dees**

Harsh Assessment
Zen Garcia
August 17, 2005

Some people may think me harsh in my assessment that the attacks in London were government sponsored terror to motivate a renewed push for the global war on terrorism. Even if it were supposedly Al-Qaeda in Europe, Al-Qaeda everywhere else is supported by the CIA and other intelligence organizations. A simple example of this is when the Taliban leaders were flown out of Afghanistan just as Special Forces were getting close.

Why would the White House in the least not demand the Taliban leadership hand them over if Pakistan, who is supposed to be our ally on the war on terror; is protecting them? It is because they did not want to lose their trained assets. If you check the 9/11 timeline put together by wanttoknow.com, there are numerous occasions when the Bush administration protected Al-Qaeda members, and even forced FBI officers to 'stand down' from their investigations. There are many intelligence officers which have resigned and even testified in Congressional hearings about orders to stand down.

Would you not agree that 9/11 was the greatest crime perpetuated on the American people? Why then did the White House prevent any investigation and even allowed the evidence to quickly be carted away so that no one could "prove" the official story and that those buildings went down because of being heated by fuel.

Also why was their no investigation into all the eye witness claims of explosions in the buildings claims substantiated by the Fire Department and even the recordings of Fire Department conversations? There is a lot that we don't know about the London bombing. We do know that every time the globalists lack public support for their war on terror, the public gets attacked. How convenient that this latest attack also takes the focus off of Karl Rove for outing Valerie Plame and getting a number of CIA assets killed as payback for her husband Joe Wilson disclaiming the Niger yellow cake lie. Iraq has plenty of uranium within their own boundaries. People please just learn about The Project for A New American Century which called for a new "Pearl Harbor" and an American foothold in Iraq with regime change being a driving force for war there.

> **Any serious effort at transformation must occur within the larger framework of U.S. national security strategy, military missions and defense budgets. The United States cannot simply declare a "strategic pause" while experimenting with new technologies and operational concepts. Nor can it choose to pursue a transformation strategy that would decouple American and allied interests. A transformation strategy that solely pursued capabilities for projecting force from the United States, for example, and sacrificed forward basing and presence, would be at odds with larger American policy goals and would trouble American allies. Further, the process of transformation, even if it brings revolutionary change, is likely to be a long one, absent some catastrophic and catalyzing event – like a new Pearl Harbor.** - Project for the New American Century

- **David Dees**

London Bombs
Zen Garcia
September 7, 2005

Government sponsored terror? Within hours it is reported that "former Israeli Prime Minister and current Finance Minister, Benjamin Netanyahu, was in London this morning for an economic forum. "Just before the first blast, Netanyahu got a call from the Israeli Embassy telling him to stay in his hotel room. The hotel is located next to the subway station where the first attack occurred and he did stay put and shortly after that, there was the explosion," Preston said. While, at first, Israel denied the claims, now they have released a press release stating that they gave the British government warning days earlier about an impending terrorist attack in London. David Shayler, a former MI5 officer from British intelligence claims that the Israeli government has been involved in terrorist attacks in London prior, blowing up their own embassy and then framing it on two young Palestinians, just so they could have reason to beef up security of their embassies across the world.

Israel controls and uses Hamas to further agenda, as the British had high intelligence operatives committing terrorist acts through the IRA, and that the CIA and MI6 use Al-Qaeda as an asset to further their agenda. They are able, through the control of both sides of the duality, to create and fund both sides of whatever war they want to create. That is why it is absolutely imperative that all people everywhere learn about this power structure or otherwise be used as pawns within their wars. With such power, how do we bring it down?

The answer lies in the process of sharing and disseminating truth. There are a very few people at the top of the Illuminati/New World Order pyramid that control the unfolding agenda of the global elite. Most of the people making up the body of the pyramid have no idea that they are being used to push a globalist one world government sponsored terror agenda all across the world. At some point a time will come when, upon learning about the actual power structure controlling the various intelligence organizations and their funded terrorist allies; that intelligence officers can only continue their work with the knowledge that they are committing atrocities and spilling innocent blood; they can quietly retire or become whistleblowers, sharing their knowledge of the agenda with the public domain, in turn protecting their own lives.

Each day more and more whistle blowers are coming into the public arena and sharing full disclosure about their insights and angles on government sponsored terror. If it were not for these great humanitarian patriots, we would not even know the things we know and would not be in this space of turning the tide. The more and more people come out with their stories, the more and more those who are naively part of the unfolding Illuminati agenda come to understand what it is they are a part of. The various officials, officers, and government employees of the various nations, truly love their countries and want nothing more than to protect their citizens and their national interests. Most have always had good intentions and well meaning aspirations, but did not know the various intelligence agencies were/are funded and run by the global elite for the benefit of fascism. Now that they are able to clearly see that there are just a handful of people pushing for one world government and the end of national sovereignty, they can speak out and expose the Bildeberger plan to unite all nations under the United Nations and global government. Praise God that the European Unions' constitution was struck down in France and the Netherlands. This was a critical defeat for the New World Order because it threw a giant monkey wrench into their push for centralization of power through the various unions of nations. The Bildeberger's are now afraid that their agenda will not be successful and that they will not be able to control the world through a United Nations free standing army and advent of global taxes.

The world spoke for peace and the end of poverty through music and the coming together of millions of people in harmony, love, and celebration through Live 8. The Illuminati needed to put the spotlight back on the war on terror and what happened - murder and mayhem in and under the streets of London. We have just learned that at the same time and on the same day of those bombings, the police were conducting a drill in which they were preparing for the exact same configuration of terrorist attacks that took place on that fateful day. Coincidence, I think not. Especially in considering that the same exact thing happened on September 11th in this country with NORAD staging war games in which planes were to be flown into various buildings across our country.

People are demanding a withdrawal of forces from Iraq and Afghanistan in Britain, America, and all across the world, especially in light of all the Downing Street Memos and undeniable knowledge that the facts would have to be fixed around the war to protect British soldiers from war crimes prosecution.
I project the movement of peace to continue and the demand for human and civil rights to increase. Too many people know what is going on and are sharing their truth on a daily basis with others who, too have decided to stand for truth. Support for their agenda can only erode as their deception is exposed further. Even though the Illuminati have forced illegal wars on Iraq and Afghanistan, they still want war with Iran Lebanon and Syria. Pray for peace.

- **David Dees**

Peace on Earth
Zen Garcia
October 24, 2005

I like you want peace to reign on the Earth and for all people to treat each other with the respect, compassion, and kindness that all people want and truly deserve. It's one of those inalienable rights that God grants to all creatures when they come into existence. For most people all they want is to grow up in spiritual, mental, emotional, and physical health. Most desire to fall in love with someone special and then hopefully raise children so that these same desired elements can be shared with offspring which can then pass what they have learned with their own children wishing the same benefit to all generations to follow. We cherish our families and love our children. Most of us can only understand war as a last resort to protect our loved ones, liberties, freedoms, and our countries. Most of us would never dream about hurting another individual, who like us have families and children they worry about and desire only the best for. Most would never ever dream of killing people in any part of our lifetime. With this in mind how can we explain all the wars, terror, oppression, slavery, genocide, and decimation of peoples during the evolution of history on our planet. Some will say yes we desire those things but only for our people. Wars of conquest and empire have through history been justified as taming those savage beasts, the second class human does not even have a soul it has been said and used as a basis for savagery that can only be defined but what it is and that is the vilest of evils.

There has always been holy texts and teachers revered by cultures that profess love for self and all others. We are told not to kill and to treat others as we would wish to be treated. So does the world only want to be killed as this is the reality that we are seeing the groundwork laid out for. A third 'crusader war' is being plotted by the Globalists that have been using war as a pretext to scare the citizens of all nations into surrendering freedoms and liberties for State protection and security. There will be greater horror than has ever been known by humankind if the globalists are not stopped in their pursuit of a one world government where all nations are equally weak and inhabited by small populations unable to shake of tyranny because of the control grid being set-up now all over the planet.

Our citizen complacency is threatening the world as America is being used as a tool to create havoc much as Hitler did until other countries have no choice but to make alliances which will eventually mean the downfall of our once great nation, followed by a massive population cull, which then can be managed by the remaining United Nations 'Peace Keeping' forces already amassed in our country. Did you know that when Hitler invaded Poland after claiming they attacked first much like America claimed Viet Nam did in the Gulf of Tonkin (both lies), and then started exterminating the Jews there; the massive camps had already been built and in place waiting for the slaughter.

Well if you investigate all the base closings, national guard and reserves being shipped overseas, and all of the closed bases being turned into empty FEMA camps scattered all over our country manned by 'foreign troops', something really fishy starts to become clear. Place that info with all the 'martial law' measures enacted and put into place by various Presidents and Congress something even more sinister becomes even that much clearer. The only thing preventing the full overthrow of our country and dictatorial martial law being implemented in our country is because we have the most armed citizenry in the world. They will have to create some kind of false flag terrorist event in order to rid of us our guns.

America must be vigilant and wake up to the very real possibility of that happening to our country. Mark my words, what is being done to the world in our name will one day return to haunt us. If we do not soon stand together and limit government, we will reap what they sow. Torture will come home. Let's hold our leaders accountable, impeach, and sentence them for the war crimes they have committed on world. If we do not do this, America will fail as the Globalists are planning its destruction. Get wise to the Bildeberger agenda. Our lives and our children's lives depend on you turning off the TV and the mindless entertainment that keeps you ignorant of what is truly going on. We are hated already all over the world. Just so you know how long America has been asleep, in 1913 Congress gave up its right and power to coin money to a privately owned European central bank under the guise of the Federal Reserve system which is neither federal nor a reserve.

Our money is no longer backed by gold. It is mass produced whenever they feel need to print and lend to our country at high interest. For this system to have been kept in place this long, let's you know how asleep this country has been and how dangerous it is for the citizenry to not be vigilant. Did you know that income taxes are illegal and that the 14th amendment was never ratified by the States and yet they have been able to cover this up just like they did 9-11 and all the other acts of terror imposed upon the population to drive agenda. America quit being the fool.

- David Dees

Awake Shake Dreams From Your Hair
Zen Garcia
January 11, 2006

There are many things which I must attempt to make the world aware of as we are about to enter a period of time which I believe threatens the current world peace. I will go through progressive steps to slowly expose the chilling truths I have uncovered as part of my own discovery of a global network of secret societies tied to certain royal bloodlines which are pushing a police state control grid to quickly bring in a one world government ruled by the United Nations. In order for them to succeed they must bring America to her knees as no nation can be powerful enough to not need the support of the United Nations.

Currently the Globalist elite are busy making the world hate Americans so they can push the world into another global thermonuclear war. All of these things have been predicted by the Bible and wherever possible I will use scripture to enlighten you further about the nature of things I talk about. It is important that you learn about the Report From iron Mountain which became the first leaked memos on the planned global depopulation agenda. In the report it talks about using vaccines, food, and water as a means to achieve depopulation. The global elite want to rid the world of 85% of its current population so that when the one world government police state is firmly entrenched around the populace, population levels will be easily manageable and a cinch to cull.

> Until now, the world we've known has been a world divided – a world of barbed wire and concrete block, conflict and cold war.
>
> Now, we can see a new world coming into view. A world in which there is the very real prospect of a new world order. In the words of Winston Churchill, a "world order" in which "the principles of justice and fair play ... protect the weak against the strong ..." A world where the United Nations, freed from cold war stalemate, is poised to fulfil the historic vision of its founders. A world in which freedom and respect for human rights find a home among all nations.
>
> The Gulf war put this new world to its first test, and, my fellow Americans, we passed that test. - George H. W. Bush Speech, March 6, 1991

- David Dees

**Record Defense Budget, Tax Cuts for the Wealthy Could =
Death for Many Americans Dependent on Medicaid Medicare
March 9, 2006
Zen Garcia**

People with disabilities are increasingly being put at risk by the Bush administrations focus on funding the 'war on terror' and the development of a 'police state' in America. "While the Pentagon budget is soaring, the Center on Budget and Policy Priorities, warns that President Bush is proposing to make cuts in hundreds of domestic programs. This includes education programs, environmental protection programs, numerous programs to assist low-income families, children, and elderly and disabled people, and research related to cancer, heart disease, and other medical conditions. In one case, the Center estimates 420,000 low-income seniors will lose food assistance from the Commodity Supplemental Food Program." The 'war on terror' while bankrupting this country, is doing nothing to protect our domestic borders, and is simply fueling the terrorists and providing them with massive recruitment opportunities especially when you take into account the torture being perpetuated on Muslims as a 'tool' in this war on terror. Homeland Security did nothing to aide Americans during Hurricane Katrina, but when it comes to establishing a police state here at home; they are striping Americans of our constitutionally guaranteed rights and civil protections in the name of security. The President's warrantless authorization for NSA to spy on Americans (mostly anti-war groups which lets you know who the government thinks the enemy is) is currently being hotly debated in congressional hearings as the executive branch tries to establish dictatorial powers overthrowing constitutional balance in the various branches of government. 52% of Americans like me are calling for IMPEACHMENT.

Most important to Bush Jr is funding wars of occupation which the American people were purposefully deceived and tricked by lies into supporting. We should be impeaching the President over his refusal to explain the Downing Street Memo not authorizing further funding especially when it is now known that over 8.8 billion dollars of tax-payers money simply disappeared and ten's of hundreds of millions of dollars were squandered through elaborate schemes to defraud the American tax-payer and the Iraqi citizens who were supposed to benefit from our assistance.

The Pentagon budget for the financial year beginning on 1 October boosts current spending on defense by 6.9 percent, bringing the total amount spent on the military to a record $439.3 billion. Under the proposed budget, defense spending will increase nearly 7 percent to $440 billion. If approved the Pentagon's budget will become 45 percent larger than when Bush took office five years ago. One recent estimate put the cost of the Iraq war at $100,000 every minute.

In 2 reports one by Truth-Out the other by MSNBC details of elaborate plots to defraud American tax-payers and Iraqi recipients include an agent who kept almost $700,000 in unexplained cash in an unlocked footlocker, an assistant to the U.S. military coach for an Iraqi sports team gambled away as much as $60,000 in reconstruction funds in the Philippines, little oversight over an oil pipeline repair contract resulted in more than $3 million in overcharges, including billing for work not done.

Other details include how investigators reviewed 43 contracts and found 29 had incomplete or missing documentation. For each of the 29, "We were unable to determine if the goods specified in the contract were ever received, the total amount of payments made to the contractor or if the contractor fully complied with the terms of the contract." An example cited, a contract for 15 double-cab pickup trucks for an Iraqi police department paid $87,500 before the trucks were delivered and an additional $100,000 without getting written records that the trucks arrived at the police department. In an article called "Staggering Amount of Cash Missing in Iraq" Three U.S. Senators have called on Defense Secretary Donald Rumsfeld to account for 8.8 billion dollars entrusted to the Coalition Provisional Authority (CPA) in Iraq that is now missing. They pointed to "disturbing findings" from the inspector general's report that the payrolls of some Iraqi ministries, then under CPA control, were padded with thousands of ghost employees. They refer to an example in which CPA paid the salaries of 74,000 security guards although the actual number of employees could not be validated. The report says that in one case some 8,000 guards were listed on a payroll but only 603 real individuals could be counted.

Haliburton overbilled American tax-payers $199 million dollars charging $50 dollars an hour to employees paid less than $5 dollars an hour in Iraq. Investigators looking into Haliburton fraud in Iraq could not track down 52 of 164 randomly selected items in an inventory of more than 20,000 items overseen by KBR, a subsidiary of Haliburton. The missing items included two electric generators worth nearly $1 million, 18 trucks or sport utility vehicles and six laptop computers. Auditors were unable to account for $97 million of the $120 million in Iraqi oil revenues earmarked for rebuilding projects. We are wasting tens of hundreds of millions probably billions if not trillions of dollars in occupying Iraq and Afghanistan when it is clear we are not wanted there(Iraqi poll Afghani poll) and even our troops on the ground do not support the war with 1/3 calling for immediate withdrawal; all the while our borders remain wide open with terrorists elements killing Americans right here in our own country but where is the mainstream media reports on this?

Both the trade deficit and national debts are now at record all time highs, the wars we have found our nation pursuing risk bankrupting our nation. This President has borrowed more money than all other President's combined. Bush has declared a war on the American poor and middle class, calling for a reduction in 'non-discretionary spending' while at the same time increasing Defense spending to record levels. People with disabilities are being forced into poverty, starvation, and death while the Pentagon and Defense Department don't even have to account for the billions of dollars they squander. What makes these claims even worse is that this has been an ongoing trend for the Pentagon who had a Trillion dollars missing in 2003. While people with disabilities die from lack of wealth for food, shelter, and health care; the government wastes money which could prolong the quality of life for millions of Americans who suffer right here in our own country.

Junior Bush claims he will spur the economy by making permanent the tax-cuts he proposed back in 2001. However careful study of making permanent the proposed tax-cuts benefit only the wealthiest of Americans. In an article entitled "The Cost of Tax Cuts" put out by 2 senior economists at the Brookings Institute shows how detrimental the effects will be to our countries revenue intake and how the brunt of these tax-breaks will be deferred to the working class. William G. Gale and Peter R. Orszag claim, "Making the tax cuts permanent would generate large, back-loaded revenue losses over the next 10 years. Combined with a minimal but necessary fix to the government's Alternative Minimum Tax, making the tax cuts permanent would reduce federal revenues by almost $1.8 trillion over 10 years - and that's in addition to the $1.7 trillion of revenue losses already locked into law. By 2014, the annual revenue loss would amount to $400 billion, or 2 percent of gross domestic product - almost the size of this year's federal budget deficit."

"Paying for the tax cuts would require monumental reductions in spending or increases in other taxes. To offset the revenue losses in 2014 would require, for example, a 48 percent reduction in Social Security benefits, a 57 percent cut in Medicare benefits, or a 117 percent increase in corporate taxes. Over the long run, making the tax cuts permanent would cost as much as repairing the shortfalls in the Social Security and Medicare Hospital Insurance trust funds. Thus, to the extent that Social Security and Medicare are considered major long-term fiscal problems, making the tax cuts permanent should be seen as creating a fiscal problem of equivalent magnitude. Making the tax cuts permanent would be regressive; that is, it would confer by far the biggest benefits on high-income taxpayers. Once plausible methods of financing the tax cuts are taken into account, more than three-quarters of households are likely to end up worse off than they would have been if the tax cuts had never taken effect."

They end their Report with, "The 2001 tax cut was a centerpiece of President Bush's electoral campaign in 2000, and much of the 2003 tax cut was a partial acceleration of the 2001 tax cut. Now the administration proposes making these tax cuts permanent. It is astonishing that, more than four years after the proposal was first made public, the administration has still not released an analysis of the plan's long-term economic effects, or even a statement of how it intends to pay for the tax cuts. Even supporters of the tax cut would presumably like to know the answers to those questions."

The President's just released 2007 year budget recommends at least a 5 percent increase for Homeland Security up from this year's funding of $30.8 billion. Similarly, the budget will contain an increase of nearly 5 percent in the Pentagon's funding for next year. The $439.3 billion includes $84.2 billion for weapons systems, an 8 percent increase in weapons spending. Not wanting to limit the scope of his budget, estimates do not even include the military expenditures being expended in the wars in Iraq and Afghanistan, with the Pentagon announcing it intends to ask Congress for an additional $120 billion -- not contained in the new spending plan -- to help pay for the wars this year and next.

Both Medicare and Medicaid are being slashed significantly putting at risk people with disabilities and the poorest of the poor. Medicare spending is being reduced by $36 billion by 2011 -- and by $105 billion a decade from now. About $20 billion of the $36 billion would come from reducing automatic payment increases to hospitals and other institutional providers, such as ambulance services and skilled-nursing facilities, while the rest would be spread among other forms of care. The Medicare spending slowdown over the next 5 years Bush envisions is larger than the $6.4 billion in Medicare reductions that Congress approved after intense political fighting, in the current year's budget. Medicaid, Congress agreed would be cut by $4.7 billion, less than half what the White House requested last year.

The Government Accountability Office (GAO) at the behest of Veterans? Affairs Chairman Steve Buyer (R-Ind.), reported findings that found unrealistic assumptions, errors in estimates, insufficient data, and an unresponsive budget model contributed to health care funding shortfalls at the Department of Veterans Affairs in fiscal years 2005 and 2006. Certain categories of care that required additional funding not included in the initial budget recommendations for the VA, were care for returning veterans of the war on terror, funding for long-term care, and care for higher priority patients essentially those who have service-connected disabilities, have special disabilities, such as spinal cord injuries, and the indigent. Learning of these and other shortfalls, Chairman Buyer began the effort that provided VA $1.5 billion in supplemental funding for 2005, with unused funds available for this year. The VA was unable to use the sum total of appropriations requested and therefore rolled over more than a billion dollars into 2006. I have heard from Veteran's on the ground here in the States that the VA is denying veterans care. Let them know that you know they have a surplus and see what they say.

In a press briefing at the Pentagon, U.S. Defense Secretary Donald Rumsfeld said the record amount allocated for defense in the 2007 budget proposal submitted to Congress on 6 February would be used to boost the United States' ability to both fight unconventional terrorism and win conventional wars. "The President's budget request for the Department of Defense represents an increase over last year. It reflects what we believe should be the country's national-security priorities, namely to help defend the United States of America and the American people and their interests, to give flexibility to commanders, to prepare for both conventional and unconventional or irregular warfare, and, importantly, to work closely with partner nations." However, what he did not say was that most Americans feel we are less safe now than before September 11th happened and that the war on terrorism as it is being fought right now does nothing more than breed terrorism and set-up the conditions which only increase terrorism world-wide. Just look at what is happening on the border here in the states.

Americans must demand oversight and an accurate accounting of the money the government has and is using to combat the war on terror. We must absolutely push Congress to bring the troops home and detox them from the depleted uranium that will eventually slaughter mercilessly most Gulf War II vets. We must also make the government honor supporting the many children being born with disabilities from these Vets. Then with the money diverted away from bankrupting wars, we must address our national debt, equalize our trade deficit, and address the severe health-care crisis here in America as well as immediately secure our borders. I will list just a few articles here to show you how dire the situation on the border is. Only in stopping these illegal wars and protecting our borders can we begin to do the things we need to here in our own country to truly insure safety. Call Congress make them sign on to John Conyers attempt at censuring King George and his Neo-con Hawks. Do it before we completely lose constitutional protections and civil rights. Ben Franklin said, "Those who would give up liberty for security, deserve neither liberty nor security."

> **In order that the masses themselves may not guess what they are about WE FURTHER DISTRACT THEM WITH AMUSEMENTS, GAMES, PASTIMES, PASSIONS, PEOPLE'S PALACES.... SOON WE SHALL BEGIN THROUGH THE PRESS TO PROPOSE COMPETITIONS IN ART, IN SPORT IN ALL KINDS: these interests will finally distract their minds from questions in which we should find ourselves compelled to oppose them.** Protocols of the Learned Elders of Zion, 13:3

-David Dees

Liar President Places America at Risk Again
April 29, 2006
Zen Garcia

President Bush has continually stressed his hard line approach to National Security and the war on terror, promising to protect the American people at all costs and with whatever tools deemed necessary. He claims above the law authority to do whatever it takes to secure America including breech of international laws and violation of our own Constitution. When confronted with statements Libby made to a federal grand jury that he had received "approval from the President through the Vice President" to leak portions of a National Intelligence Estimate including Valerie Plame Wilson's covert identity as a way of defending the Bush administration's decision to go to war with Iraq, and as an attempt to silence war critic Ambassador Joe Wilson; Scott McClellan in response said, "The President believes the leaking of classified information is a very serious matter. And I think that's why it's important to draw a distinction here. Declassifying information and providing it to the public, when it is in the public interest, is one thing. But leaking classified information that could compromise our national security is something that is very serious. And there is a distinction."

He attempted to illustrate this distinction by pointing to the leaking of the existence of the warrantless NSA spying program to the press by someone, McClellan claims put our National security at risk because it had informed Al-Qaeda that we were snooping on their international calls to the U.S. However, contrary to his claims it has been known since 1998 that "Bin Laden and his lieutenants quit using satellite phones the day after a cruise missile attack by the Clinton administration on a facility in Sudan because it was known that the United States was eavesdropping on their calls." Al-Qaeda since that time uses only encrypted phone calls and E-mail messages. "Calls are also hard to trace. One government official explains: 'A guy buys 10 or 15 cellphones' services, and the minute he thinks we might be on to him, he throws it away.' Forsaking legitimate banks, al Qaeda moves its money through a network of underground exchangers." Even Time magazine reported in September 24, 2001, that Bin Laden "had already quit using his satellite phone because its signal can be traced."

Thanks to documents released by the ACLU, we know that the real target of the warrantless spying being carried out by the NSA, is the antiwar groups here in America opposed to the current administration's corrupt, immoral, and criminal war in Iraq. Whereas leaking of the NSA program to the press may have endanger our country's National Security to some degree, I believe the White House was more concerned with disclosure of the impeachable conduct being carried out with the President's authority. McClellan said, "The President of the United States has the authority to declassify information. I also indicated to some reporters earlier today that the President would never authorize the disclosure of information that he felt could compromise our nation's security."

And yet the leaking of Valerie Plame's covert identity truly did place this country in grave danger and may have even lead to the death of a covert CIA agent associated to Valerie Plame Wilson. Wayne Madsen, a reporter and former NSA employee, has claimed, "CIA sources report that at least one anonymous star placed on the CIA's Wall of Honor at its Langley, Virginia headquarters is a clandestine agent who was executed in a hostile foreign nation as a direct result of the White House leak." For those who have not followed or do not understand the intricacies behind the Valerie Plame case, I will revisit the story so that in understanding this, you will see how the Bush administration put this country and many of our covert agents at risk, all just to get back at Ambassador Wilson for debunking the Niger uranium story. Please reaffirm for yourself what I am about to reveal to you.

First, I'd like to state that Iraq has within its borders significant quantities of uranium and would not need to purchase yellow cake from outside sources. "Because Iraq has natural uranium deposits, all they need to do is build a process to enrich that uranium to weapons grade and then enrich enough to make one or more Hiroshima-sized weapons." said Kenneth M. Pollack, in his book "The Threatening Storm." This fact has been further corroborated by certain declassified portions of a 2002 National Intelligence Estimate, "Iraq possesses significant phosphate deposits, from which uranium had been chemically extracted before Operation Desert Storm. Intelligence information on whether nuclear-related phosphate mining and/or processing has been reestablished is inconclusive."

Ambassador Joseph Wilson, had been involved in international politics for more than 20 years at the time that his wife Valerie Plame Wilson was outed by the Bush administration. He was the acting U.S. Ambassador to Iraq during Operation Desert Shield and was the last American official to meet with Saddam Hussein prior to the first invasion. In 2002 at the behest of Vice-president

Cheney, Mr. Wilson was assigned to the CIA to investigate whether Saddam Hussein had been seeking uranium from Niger for the purpose of advancing Iraq's nuclear program. The Bush administration was trying desperately to drum up support for their claims that America was in imminent danger. Most of the assessments being provided by the intelligence communities did not support their claims, and with little evidence they were desperate to keep alive those few rumors that still did exist. They were basing their trumped up threat assessment on basically 4 stories - 1) the Niger procurement story, 2) the aluminum tubes story, and 3) the mobile biological, nuclear, chemical lab story and 4) an allegation by Czech intelligence that Atta had met with an Iraqi intelligence officer in Prague in April 2001. All statements since have been proven to be false.

Ambassador Wilson having had a special relationship with the Nigerian government went to Africa to verify whether the allegations brought forth by the Bush administration, that Iraq was indeed trying to procure uranium from Niger, had any truth to it. He found the story to be baseless and upon returning from Africa, Wilson filed a report stating so. He never expected to hear anything further about the report until he heard President Bush repeat the Niger claims in his 2003 State of the Union address even though it had been removed from several drafts of his previous speeches. Ambassador Wilson not believing the President used the Niger procurement story in his speech, and then wrote a New York Times op-ed piece asserting that the Bush administration was overly exaggerating the case for an invasion of Iraq. It was at that time that the White House began scheming on how to discredit Ambassador Wilson, first assassinating his character, and then by publicly outing the covert identity of his wife Valerie Plame, a clandestine CIA operative. The White House desired to make an example out of Wilson to others that might also attempt to challenge the administration; and like a playground bully, Wilson's wife was outed as revenge for debunking the Niger procurement story.

While McClellan claims, "it was in the public interest that (this) information be declassified," the administration's actions outing Valerie Plame, placed this nation at grave risk especially considering the kind of covert work Valerie Plame did for our country. Valerie Plame was an undercover CIA agent that worked covertly for Brewster Jennings and Associates. Brewster Jennings was a well-established CIA proprietary company that worked specifically on removing illicit black market weapons of mass destruction, by purchasing them off of the streets, and delivering them to a secure site where they were dismantled rendering them useless. She was part of an operation tracking distribution and acquisition of weapons of mass destruction technology to and from Iran. "Speaking under strict confidentiality, intelligence officials revealed heretofore unreported elements of Plame's work. Their accounts suggest that Plame's outing was more serious than has previously been reported and carries grave implications for U.S. National security and its ability to monitor Iran's burgeoning nuclear program. While many have speculated that Plame was involved in monitoring the nuclear proliferation black market, specifically the proliferation activities of Pakistan's nuclear 'father,' A.Q. Khan, intelligence sources say that her team provided only minimal support in that area, focusing almost entirely on Iran."

"Several intelligence officials described the damage in terms of how long it would take for the agency to recover. According to their own assessment, the CIA would be impaired for up to "ten years" in its capacity to adequately monitor nuclear proliferation on the level of efficiency and accuracy it had prior to the White House leak of Plame Wilson's identity." There is speculation from Wayne Madsen, a reporter and former NSA employee, who wrote on July 2, 2005, "CIA sources report that at least one anonymous star placed on the CIA's Wall of Honor at its Langley, Virginia headquarters is a clandestine agent who was executed in a hostile foreign nation as a direct result of the White House leak." Whether this is true or not, just the fact that the administration blew the cover of myriad's of America's covert CIA agents working to prevent Iran from garnering material which could be used in constructing a nuclear weapon, does not make sense when taking into account Bush's so called stance on national security and rhetoric towards Iran on enriching uranium.

This should inform America on the dangers of our allowing this President and his entire cover-up administration to remain in office. This administration is dangerous to the safety and protection of the American people. The borders are still wide open; our military is stretched so thin that we couldn't counter another threat if we wanted to. Our nation risks going bankrupt due to the frivolous spending of Bush as he has already borrowed more money than all other Presidents combined. The outing of Valerie Plame Wilson by the White House in 2003 for political gain caused significant damage to U.S. National security and its ability to counter nuclear proliferation abroad. America does not yet fully understand how and to what extent we as a public and our intelligence apparatus were put at risk, however it is absolutely clear to even average Americans struggling just to survive, that this President holds no credentials at all to be trusted further with any matter important to America. Bush said, "If there's a leak out of my administration, I want to know who it is. If the person has violated law, that person will be taken care of. I welcome the investigation. I am absolutely confident the Justice Department will do a good job. I want to know the truth. Leaks of classified information are bad things." He also said that he did not know of "anybody in my administration who leaked classified information" and that he told his administration to "cooperate fully with the investigation and asked anyone with knowledge of the case to come forward." He even made his staff go through an ethics class after the leak was reported.

Isn't it passed due that we impeach this criminal President. How can we trust him to defend our nation when he violates international law, our Constitution, and places us in grave danger by following a unilateral declaration of preemptive war, CIA sanctioned kidnapping, and torture. When will the rest of America join John Bonifaz, a lawyer for the Center for Constitutional Rights call to impeach Bush. "The President of the United States has been actively engaged in a conspiracy to deceive and mislead the United States Congress and the American people about the basis for going to war against Iraq. If true, such conduct constitutes a High Crime under Article II, Section 4 of the United States Constitution: The President, Vice President, and all civil officers of the United States shall be removed from office on impeachment for, and conviction of, treason, bribery, or other high crimes and misdemeanors." George Herbert Walker Bush said in 1991 at the dedication of the George Bush CIA headquarters, "Even though I'm a tranquil guy now at this stage of my life, I have nothing but contempt and anger for those who betray the trust by exposing the name of our sources. They are, in my view, the most insidious of traitors." Little did he know his own son would be this most 'insidious of traitors' and as an insidious traitor he needs to be impeached and removed from office before he places our nation at even greater risk. "The fact that the president was willing to reveal classified information for political gain and put the interests of his political party ahead of America's security shows that he can no longer be trusted to keep America safe," said Democratic National Committee Chairman Howard Dean

> When we at last definitely come into our kingdom by the aid of COUPS D'ETAT prepared everywhere for one and the same day, after definitely acknowledged we shall make it our task to see that against us such things as plots shall no longer exist. With this purpose we shall slay without mercy all who take arms to oppose our coming into our kingdom. Every kind of new institution of anything like a secret society will also be punished with death; those of them which are now in existence, are known to us, serve us and have served us, we shall disband and send into exile to continents far removed from Europe. IN THIS WAY WE SHALL PROCEED WITH THOSE *"GOY"* MASONS WHO KNOW TOO MUCH; such of these as we may for some reason spare will be kept in constant fear of exile. - The Protocols of the Learned Elders of Zion, 15:1

-David Dees

Support Our Troops - Tell Them the Truth

July 28, 2006
Zen Garcia

What I want to know is who is going to protect this country, should our country nuke Iran and plunge us into the next global war? We do not even have a large civilian defense force present in the country to protect our home front as most are in Iraq. This vulnerability was perfectly illustrated by the Katrina disaster and the abandonment of hundreds of thousands of American citizens on American soil, all in desperate need for critical basic life necessities which their government, leadership failed to provide. Many died in the streets awaiting help that was yet days away. Bush and lackeys must not have considered the drowning of one of America's greatest cities an important enough cause to end their month long sabbaticals as they did not even disrupt their vacations to address the onrushing threat of what turned out to be the greatest natural disaster to ever hit American soil.

The National Guard troops that should be protecting our homeland are in Iraq, breathing the same depleted uranium killing our active military. It is just a matter of time before all of our troops begin dying from the mysterious Gulf War syndrome that military doctors inside the US cannot declare cause of, but doctors outside the military have determined to be depleted uranium poisoning. Our troops are not going to be able to take care of themselves much less defend our nation, protect the common good, from fascist interests domestic and abroad. At some point our nation will have to own up to the horrible truth that the leadership poisoned our own troops. Once the grunts on the field understand that the President and military leaders sacrificed them like a sin offering, who then will ever join our military to defend our nation? How could soldiers in the field ever trust leadership that lied about reasons for going to war and then endangered their lives by not telling them the dangers of depleted uranium use. It is unconscionable that our military leadership has known since 1943 that depleted uranium weaponry would be grossly harmful to our own ground soldiers as well as the civilian population that remains behind long after the battle is waged.

A declassified memo (written by James B. Conant and two other physicists working on the U.S. nuclear project during the Second World War) sent to Brig. Gen. L.R. Groves on October 30, 1943, proves our government's accountability. "As a gas warfare instrument the [radioactive] material would be ground into particles of microscopic size to form dust and smoke and distributed by a ground-fired projectile, land vehicles, or aerial bombs," the 1943 memo reads. "In this form it would be inhaled by personnel. The amount necessary to cause death to a person inhaling the material is extremely small. It has been estimated that one millionth of a gram accumulation in a person's body would be fatal. There are no known methods of treatment for such a casualty."

If our leaders really wanted to support our troops, they would come clean on the realities and horrors of depleted uranium usage. Can you imagine how betrayed our military personnel will feel once they realize the leadership condemned them to die horrible deaths unless they all get detoxed from exposure to this nuclear waste which the Veterans Administration won't pay for or even list as a cause for symptoms. Studies of the first Gulf War veterans and the gulf war syndrome find 300,000 US veterans have been exposed to inhale DU and are excreting uranium 238 (DU) in their urine and semen. Children in countries where DU has been used (Kuwait, Bosnia, Kosovo, and Iraq) are having a higher than normal incidence of malignancies and congenital malformations. Children of Gulf War veterans exposed to DU also stand the higher than normal risk of malignancy or malformation.

The crisis only grows as we continue adding du particles into the atmosphere. Whereas Coalition Forces dropped 350 tonnes of DU in the first gulf war, 2003 estimates for the current gulf war we have dropped or shot, 1100 to 2200 tonnes of depleted uranium shells, bullets, and bombs. Unless we place pressure on the pentagon to quit using DU munitions, the whole world will be at risk as DU can travel piggyback easily into every part of the world threatening the health of all biological creatures everywhere it ends up. This stuff is so harmful that just 1 particle can lead to cancer in lung, bone, kidney, prostate, gut and brain. Here's the real shocker though, DU has a half-life of 4.5 billion years which means contamination will last until it is placed in a secure environment where it cannot harm living tissue or contaminate soil or groundwater.

Our Military and National Guard everyday return home sick and dying from exposure to depleted uranium rounds. As they suffer doctors try as they might to alleviate the pain, they cannot do much about the escalating symptoms. How does the U.S. Military view the safety of DU munitions? In a letter to Senator Sam Nunn, a representative of the U.S. Air Force stated, "...these projectiles are no more hazardous to store, transport, or employ than those composed of lead or copper" (Ref. 39). This view is echoed in the U.S. Army report to Congress that states, "The health risks associated with using DU in peacetime are minimal. This includes risks associated with transporting, storing and handling intact DU munitions and armor during peacetime" (Ref. 40). Neither the Air Force nor the Army has publicly presented an analysis of the health risks to soldiers and to others who inhale or ingest radioactive fallout particles of DU, or the health risks of living in an environment contaminated with DU after these munitions have been fired: these are the real safety issues they ignore. In the AEPI report, (Ref. 42) the Army judges it an acceptable risk if its personnel become exposed in an unprotected fashion to the combustion products of fired DU munitions on the battlefield or elsewhere

The official military stand on DU is that it does not harm soldiers. The American people must demand our government truly support our troops by bringing them home and getting them the help they absolutely need to detox, preserve their lives, and the unity of their families.

Who will ever suspect then that ALL THESE PEOPLES WERE STAGE-MANAGED BY US ACCORDING TO A POLITICAL PLAN WHICH NO ONE HAS SO MUCH AS GUESSED AT IN THE COURSE OF MANY CENTURIES?
 – The Protocols of the Learned Elders of Zion, 13:6

-David Dees

The Ghosts of 9/11
August 26, 2006
Zen Garcia

Five years ago, 3023 of our fellow citizens lost their lives in what was to be one of the most devastating atrocities to ever take place on American soil. Tatyana, my attendant woke me up and flipped me to my backside before she left for school. I turned on the news to watch the opening of the market when a friend instant messaged me and said the North Tower in New York had been struck by a Boeing 757.

I thought it must have been an accident that surely some pilot or computer malfunction made the flight veer off course and unfortunately ram into the World Trade Tower. I changed the channel to CNN when out of nowhere another airliner entered screen and disappeared into the corner of the South Tower, exiting the other side in a massive fireball. For the rest of that day week month, I found myself glued to coverage of ensuing events; flipping from news source to news source seeking as much information as was available through mainstream news, supplementing the rest with the alternative media. I had access to a local New York ABC affiliate WIXT, through satellite TV and was able to watch events largely as New Yorker's saw them for themselves.

It was a real window into the horror that the city and our nation was forced to deal with. I personally did not know anyone who died during the events of those days, but as an American, I empathized with their struggle. The whole world did. People everywhere were incredibly moved by a want to help the people who were and would be suffering for years to come. Nobody ever imagined that some force powerful enough to pull this off, would hate Americans so much as to contemplate inflicting such carnage upon the citizenry of this country. It is one thing to be at war and seek to achieve strategic victories against a military foe. It is quite another for someone to envision and purposely intend harm against innocent civilians.

It's now 5 years later and honoring the anniversary of the attacks, I present the story of William Rodriguez, a janitorial foreman responsible for the cleanup and maintenance of stairwells in World Trade Center 1, the North Tower. Rodriguez had worked his first day in the towers, exactly twenty years to the day of the attacks of September 11th, 2001. He had also survived the bombing in '93.

On that tragic morning Rodriguez found himself running 30 minutes behind for work. He called his boss, who told him to get there as soon as he could. Because he was late, he would have to go to an office in sub-basement 1 to clock in. At least 14 other people were in the office when suddenly a massive explosion occurred beneath their feet. "Seconds after the first massive explosion below in the basement, I hear another explosion from way above. Although I was unaware at the time, this was the airplane hitting the tower, it occurred moments after the first explosion."

A co-worker Felipe David stormed into the basement office with severe burns, skin hanging from his face, hands, and arms; screaming "explosion! explosion! explosion!" David had been standing in front of a freight elevator close to the office when fire followed the elevator shaft up and leapt upon him causing terrible burns. "That day I was in the basement in sub-level 1 sometime after 8:30am. Everything happened so fast, everything moved so fast. The building started shaking after I heard the explosion below, dust was flying everywhere and all of a sudden it got real hot. I threw myself onto the floor, covered my face because I felt like I was burned. I sat there for a couple of seconds on the floor and felt like I was going to die, saying to myself 'God, please give me strength,'" released David in a 2002 interview.

Had he not been late Rodriguez would have been at the top of the North Tower beginning his normal routine having breakfast with friends at the Windows of the World, a cafe at the pinnacle of the building. "It was a miracle. If I arrived on time, like always, I'd probably be dead. I would have been up at the top floors like every morning," said Rodriguez in an interview with Greg Szymanski of The American Free Press.

Rodriguez, who knew the complex very, very well, escorted David to an ambulance outside the underground facilities and then returned to show others the way out. Once he returned he found Salvatore Giambanco and another unidentified man stuck in a basement elevator. Rodriguez managed to pry open the elevator, enter the shaft, and call out to the men below, who yelled back they ere at risk of drowning - thigh high in run-off from the sprinkler systems. Rodriguez returned to the parking garage where he was able to commandeer a long extension ladder. He then maneuvered himself and the ladder into the darkened shaft of the elevator to lower the ladder down to Giambanco and the unidentified man.

Rodriguez then led these two men to safety, and was then ordered by police not to return to the North Tower. Being in charge of only one of five master keys for WTC 1, he felt his return vital in assisting emergency crews especially fire fighters in accessing the various parts of the building they would need to go to save lives some of which may be his friends. So he rushed past police heading again into the towering inferno. Once he located fire crews, he lead them upwards unlocking doors, they had been hacking through.

As they made their way up the stairwell to the 33rd floor, Rodriguez heard a series of small explosions going off between the 20th and 30th floors. Once they reached the 39th floor fire fighters told him that he must turn back because he was not an emergency worker and was endangering his own safety. The crew leader ordered him to make his descent to the 27th floor and to do what he could for a female quadriplegic they had passed on their way up. After that as soon as possible he was to get himself out of the building. As he started downward Rodriguez heard explosions from the South Tower not realizing that it had collapsed. Once he reached the 27th floor, he found an emergency crew with gurney trying to assist the woman. He helped them carry her out of the building, leaving her with an available ambulance. Shortly thereafter the North Tower began to collapse.

Had he been in the South Tower he would surely have died, although the South Tower was the 2nd building hit, it was the first to collapse 56 minutes after being struck by flight 175. At 10:28, 1 hour and 42 minutes after being struck by flight 11, the North Tower collapsed in 'demolition' uniformity at breakneck speed giving Rodriguez only time enough to dive under a fire truck. Rodriguez only hoped the truck would be strong enough to protect him from being crushed by falling debris. He survived the collapse and was later dug out by the fire crews that also survived the collapsing towers.

Rodriguez lost two hundred of his closest friends and associates on that day. He was labeled a hero by all that had encountered him and did numerous interviews with the many different news agencies, domestically and abroad. NBC spent a full day at his house taping his comments. Thinking his testimony important to enable investigators to uncover more details about the crime, he presented his story to all who would listen. He even testified before the 9-11 commission oddly enough behind closed doors. Eventually, years passed, Rodriguez never saw his tale aired on the mainstream news in America, beyond just a few second sound bites. He wasn't seeking fame and fortune, but he did have questions which to him were never fully explained like "How could a jetliner hit 90 floors above and burn a man's arms and face to a crisp in the basement below within seconds of impact?"

It soon became apparent to Rodriguez that the reason his story had not aired was because it did not corroborate the official story. The official story says that nineteen mostly Saudi terrorists, were lucky and clever enough to simultaneously hijack four flights and fly them into various targets; outwitting our trillion dollar local, state, and federal intelligence agencies. The 14 eye-witnesses that were with William on sub-basement 1 and those Rodriguez saved question the official story that jet fuel super heated steel and brought down those buildings when never in the history of fire, has any steel structured building lost structural integrity from fire alone especially in less than 1 hour as in the case of the South Tower.

Even if the official story that burning jet fuel was responsible for the toppling of the Twin Towers, it cannot explain how World Trade Center 7 collapsed when neither plane nor building had damaged it. It had only 2 very small isolated pockets of fire in it and yet at 5:20 p.m., this 48 story building folded perfectly in on itself. Nobody has yet addressed the huge explosion that occurred right before the first plane hits as confirmed by Jose Sanchez, who worked 14 years for the American Building Maintenance Co. at the WTC. He confirmed details of a basement bomb-like explosion while Rodriguez and two CNN interns, Carolina Inojosa and Evita Zerebrinsky, interviewed victims and documented information for many people having trouble getting needed government assistance after 9/11.

In the 2002 taped statement, Sanchez recalls, "It sounded like a bomb and the lights went on and off. We started to walk to the exit and a huge ball of fire went through the freight elevator. The hot air from the ball of fire dropped Chino to the floor and my hair got burned. I said 'Chino, let's go we gotta get out of here.' But Chino was wounded and told me he needed help. I remember him saying that the hot air came with such force that it broke his leg. We finally went out through another exit and his leg and knee were both broken." Sanchez helped Chino to a parking lot where Chino was driven to help.

Seismographs at Columbia University's Lamont-Doherty Earth Observatory in Palisades, N.Y., 21 miles north of the WTC, recorded seismic activity on Sept. 11 which substantiates the stories of Rodriguez and the others. While no noticeable seismic activity could be found related to the impact at the Pentagon, the Palisades seismic record shows that two unexplained spikes more than 20 times the amplitude of the other seismic waves associated with the collapses, occurred in the East-West seismic recording as the buildings began to fall. Experts cannot explain why the seismic waves peaked before the towers actually hit the ground. The strongest jolts were all registered at the beginning of the collapses, well before the falling debris struck the Earth.

Bill Manning, editor of Fire Engineering, a 125-year-old-monthly firefighting trade magazine with ties to the New York City Fire Department, wrote in an editor's opinion piece in the January 2002 issue called "$elling Out the Investigation", "Fire Engineering has good reason to believe that the 'official investigation' blessed by FEMA and run by the American Society of Civil Engineers is a half-baked farce that may already have been commandeered by political forces whose primary interests, to put it mildly, lie far afield of full disclosure." He also called for an immediate stop to the removal of steel from the site of ground zero saying the steel from the site should be preserved as a crime scene so that investigators can examine what caused the collapse and pass that knowledge on to future generations of engineers. The editorial continues, "A growing number of fire protection engineers have theorized that 'the structural damage from the planes and the explosive ignition of jet fuel in themselves were not enough to bring down the towers," the editorial stated.

Szymanski says of Rodriguez, "His eyewitness account, backed up by at least 14 people at the scene with him, isn't speculation or conjecture. It isn't a story that takes a network out on a journalistic limb. It's a story that can be backed up, a story that can be verified with hospital records and testimony from many others. It's a story about 14 people who felt and heard the same explosion and even saw Rodriguez, moments after the airplane hit, take David to safety, after he was burnt so bad from the basement explosion flesh was hanging from his face and both arms." Rodriguez continues to work to educate the American public and will go on a speaking tour sometime soon throughout the United States. He says that he has been told many times to keep quiet. Rodriguez claims he should have died on that fateful day, but was spared and because he was spared, he says he must speak for the 200 friends who lost their voice and their lives on that fateful day.

-David Dees

The Torture King and Loss of Habeas Corpus
September 27, 2006
Zen Garcia

Bush has stated over and over, "We do not torture detainees" and yet when Senator McCain, a once held prisoner of war, dissented against the White House position on the treatment of detainees and together with the Senate passed a law outlawing the torture of detainees; Bush issued a 'signing statement' - an official document in which a president lays out interpretation of a new law -in which he reserved the right to ignore Congressional demands outlawing the torture of prisoners.

He claims authority as commander in chief to bypass any law, in context of broader powers to protect national security. Bush believes he can waive any restrictions which would impede his ability to protect the American people from the threats of terrorism. "The executive branch shall construe [the law] in a manner consistent with the constitutional authority of the President...as Commander in Chief... in achieving the shared objective of the Congress and the President...of protecting the American people from further terrorist attacks."

Bush had stated on numerous occasions not only that America does not torture detainees, but that America is not running black sites in which detainees are flown to some obscure location where the rule of law does not exist so that extreme measures can be used to excise information it deems necessary to protecting our citizenry. Having had the program of extraordinary rendition called into question by several federal judges, the White House has had to fess up to the existence of such a program. "I cannot describe the specific methods used - I think you understand why," Bush said during a 5th anniversary speech of the attacks of September 11th. "If I did, it would help the terrorists learn how to resist questioning, and to keep information from us that we need to prevent new attacks on our country. But I can say the procedures were tough, and they were safe, and lawful and necessary."

He reiterated his insistence that detainees have not and will not be tortured, claiming "I want to be absolutely clear with our people, and the world: The United States does not torture. It's against our laws, and it's against our values. I have not authorized it, and I will not authorize it." What the world and Americans do not realize is that what we the people traditionally consider torture, is not the same torture Bush speaks about since attorney general Alberto Gonzales redefined torture in a narrow context. The Torture Convention defines torture as "any act by which severe pain or suffering, whether physical or mental, is intentionally inflicted on a person".

The Bush Administration declares torture by a different standard, namely that, to constitute torture, the pain caused "must be equivalent in intensity to the pain accompanying serious physical injury, such as organ failure, impairment of bodily functions or even death." Methods generally understood by the world as "torture" would be permitted by this newly and narrowly altered definition. According to the new 'definition' everything up to the point leading to death is not torture as defined by the Administrations new policy. The redefining of torture, allows the administration to deny criminal behavior while still allowing the implementation and committing of such atrocities. This also gave CIA and military interrogators the 'go-ahead' to try many drastic measures considered too tough in previous sessions prior to the 'war on terror.'

Bush wants the CIA to be exempt from prosecution under the war crimes act for cruel and inhumane treatment of detainees and is now hard at work propagandizing the American public and Congress to have the Geneva Conventions modified. He knows that his administration has committed war crimes against humanity, which he and many members of his administration are liable to be prosecuted under according to international law. If he can exempt the CIA from such prosecutions then not only can they continue this sinister program of kidnap and torture, CIA interrogators won't have to worry about future prosecution, or holding back from current methods of gleaning information.

Even with torture being narrowly redefined, Bush is outright lying when he claims that, "We do not torture detainees." According to figures compiled by the Associated Press news agency, at least 108 people have died in US custody in Iraq and Afghanistan since 2002. The AP based their claims on information obtained from the US's own army, navy and senior administration officials. While many of the deaths were due to natural causes, as a result of insurgent attacks on US detention facilities or during violent prison uprisings in which lethal force was used by US personnel, at least 26 have been investigated as criminal homicide involving abusing prisoners to death. "Military investigators have looked into -- or are continuing to investigate -- 35 cases of alleged abuse or deaths of prisoners in detention facilities in the Central Command theater," said Army Secretary Les Brownlee.

A Pentagon report to Congressional oversight committee cited six prisoner deaths as of last September. Another report based on information from Pentagon and other official US sources, released by Human Rights First in October 2005 cites similar conclusions in that over 100 prisoners have died while in US custody in Iraq and Afghanistan since August 2002. Out of 98 deaths, at least 34 were suspected or confirmed homicides "caused by intentional or reckless behavior". Human Rights First representative Deborah Pearlstein told Newsnight she was "extremely comfortable" that the information was reliable while UK MP Bob Marshall-Andrews told the Press Association that "If it is indeed systemic, then the responsibility for it must go right to the top, and that would apply to both British and American governments."

A spokesman for Amnesty International UK called for an investigation into how the deaths occurred while in US custody and said, "Deaths in custody during the war on terror are a real matter of concern to us and we want to see the US and its allies allowing a full independent and impartial investigation into these deaths, as well as mounting incidents of alleged torture and other mistreatment."

Some methods used by the CIA and military interrogators include using a scalpel to make numerous cuts on the penis of Benyam Mohammed, who was arrested at Karachi airport on April 10 2002, and flown by a US government plane to a prison in Morocco. Other techniques include forceful beatings and even stomping which resulted in the paralysis of Sami Al-Laithi, a result of his detention at the U.S. military prison at Guantanamo Bay. Al-Laithi is now confined to a wheelchair with two broken vertebrae. Images released from the Abu Ghraib scandal show the forceful rape, sodomy of Iraqi men, women, and children and include depictions of electrical wires attached to the genitalia of detainees. There were also images of dogs being used to attack detainees. Would it shock the American people to know that John C. Yoo, a Justice Department attorney who helped devise the Bush regime's doctrine of torture, condones even the torture of terrorists' children to extract information from their terrorist parents.

When asked a hypothetical question in which the child of a terrorist suspect had their 'genitals crushed' in front of his father in order to extract information; Yoo answered there is "no law" and "no treaty" that would forbid such an atrocity, assuming that it was authorized by the president: "I think it depends on why the President thinks he needs to do that," Yoo said. How can an attorney for the Justice Department condone the torture of children, even terrorist children to safeguard the security of the American people?

We know through Seymour Hersh's work that the policy of torturing and sodomizing terrorist children had in fact been implemented because the Pentagon has videotapes of boys being sodomized at Abu Ghraib to extract information from their parents. "[There's] a massive amount of criminal wrongdoing that was covered up at the highest command out there, and higher. Basically what happened is that those women who were arrested with young boys/children in cases that have been recorded. The boys were sodomized with the cameras rolling. The worst about all of them is the soundtrack of the boys shrieking.... They are in total terror it's going to come out."

Manuals used by the U.S. Army's School of the Americas between 1982 and 1991 condoned executions, beatings and many other human rights abuses. John Yoo admits that he regards the sexual torture of children to be a legal and justifiable tactic, if authorized by the president. Louise Arbour, the United Nations High Commissioner for Human Rights, on December 7, 2005 declared: "The absolute ban on torture, a cornerstone of the international human rights edifice, is under attack. The principle we once believed to be unassailable-the inherent right to physical integrity and dignity of the person-is becoming a casualty of the so-called war on terror."

The world now knows that the torture of detainees was not a result of a few bad apples, but is and was a direct consequence of orders coming all the way from the President and relayed through the Secretary of Defense Donald Rumsfeld to troops on the ground. Why else would Bush fight so hard to legitimize his administration's stance on torture and extraordinary rendition? He and the Vice-President had lobbied congress to exempt the CIA from the McCain Bill outlawing torture by US Personnel and when they failed; Bush issued one of his infamous signing statements claiming authority to interpret the law anyway he sees fit even if it means ignoring it. We know that it is the administration that was and is responsible for implementing torture on a broad scale.

Interrogators as well as detainees have made public claims that torture does not solicit valuable information and fearing such treatment detainees will admit to anything just to have the torture stop even a former U.S. Army Interrogator describes why "Torture is the worst possible thing we can do to detainees." Bush keeps citing the criticalness of continuing this CIA program of extraordinary rendition, torture, and indefinite detention; claiming it a necessary evil in the war on terror. However, even Bush's own former Secretary of State, Colin Powell disagrees with his opinion on this matter. Powell sent a letter to Sen. John McCain, warning against Bush's proposal to allow more extreme methods of interrogating detainees. "The world is beginning to doubt the moral basis of our fight against terrorism," Powell said, adding Bush's policies on the treatment of detainees "would put our troops at risk." And it does put our troops at risk especially when the world knows that we are torturing everybody that we take into custody and using various unholy methods just to extract information. The Red Cross released a report about how 70-90% of the Abu Ghraib detainees who had been tortured were innocent. Doesn't the indiscriminate torture of people create hatred for those who commit such violations? We create terrorists by subjecting them to such terrorism as torture especially when they are innocent. What will happen to our troops when they are caught by so called enemy combatants? Do we as nation believe that our troops will be extended any kind of courtesy when we ourselves do not extend any kind of courtesy to prisoners of war?

Three key Republican Senators on the Armed Services Committee: John McCain, Lindsey Graham and John Warner have challenged the White House on this issue. The three helped pass a measure last week affirming Common Article Three of the Geneva Conventions, which prohibits inhumane treatment. Sen. Lindsey Graham told reporters after Rumsfeld testified before their committee, "The American public needs to understand we're talking about rape and murder here. We're not just talking about giving people a humiliating experience. We're talking about rape and murder -- and some very serious charges."

Newsweek magazine reported that the Bush administration is trying to maintain at least seven existing CIA interrogation methods for use against detainees including induced hypothermia; long periods of forced standing; sleep deprivation and "attention slapping." While McCain, Warner, and Graham have come out in defiance of the administration's attempt to limit common article 3 of the Geneva Convention, both bills proposed in the Senate strip away the right of habeas corpus from detainees and limits the ability of torture survivors to hold their perpetrators accountable for their abuse and to even know what charges have been filed against them.

Michael Ratner of the Center for Constitutional Rights said, "In both the administration bill and in the McCain-Graham-Warner bill, in both cases you abolish the writ of habeas corpus. The government, the Congress, is abolishing the writ of habeas corpus. The habeas corpus writ is the right to challenge your detention once you're picked up by the United States. It would apply to Guantanamo. It would apply to everybody in Bagram. And it basically says that anybody picked up, now or in the future or who is there now, no longer has the writ of habeas corpus. For some reason, for some peculiar reason, nobody is really covering this in the media. Yes, they're covering the McCain debate over waterboarding and torture and somewhat on the military commissions, but not really the denial of the abolishment of the fundamental writ. If we look at Maher Arar, his is one of the cases. I mean, there may be Maher Arars -- or are, as I know -- in places like Guantanamo and other places in the world, and without an ability to bring those cases to court, the United States can continue or the administration can continue doing what it did to Maher Arar."

The writ of habeas corpus guarantees a prisoners right to know the charges against them in a court of law without being held in indefinite confinement just because someone wants them detained. Without it Presidents and Kings have historically been able to lock people up, essentially throwing away the key, and disappearing them by allowing them to rot in jail. The writ of habeas corpus stems from the Magna Carta of 1215 and was so important for protecting peoples rights that when our forefathers wrote our Constitution in the United States, it became a foundation point for our own Bill of Rights. Having the writ of habeas corpus suspended for terror suspects, can also endanger American citizens as the Patriot Act defines 'domestic terrorists' as anyone that challenges the policies of government administration especially anti-war demonstrators.

Should the writ of habeas corpus be suspended indefinitely, it will only be a matter of time before anti-war, anti-police state, peace loving Americans like myself, yourself are locked up as a harassment measure and possibly indefinitely detained with charges considered 'state secrets.' We may then be brought before bogus 'military tribunals' where we can then be sentenced to death without every knowing or the government releasing what crime we may have committed and been sentenced to death for. If you think this is far from the truth, look into the case of Jose Padilla, an American citizen who was held without charge for 3 years on information considered 'state secret' until a federal judge expressed doubts about the strength of the government's terror conspiracy case against he and others. The judge ordered prosecutors to provide more evidence of alleged violent activities overseas because the judge could find no real concrete evidence for his prosecution or further imprisonment.

All people should be extended the same courtesies guaranteed to us by the US Constitution and International Law. The American people must realize that surrendering civil liberties, rights, and protections will not make us safer from terrorists. It only endangers us further by allowing fascism to creep into our government. We must remember that our founding fathers established our Constitutional Republic based on the knowledge that big government was the greatest purveyor of injustice against the people and individual freedoms.

Our Bill of Rights was written in such a way as to protect us from tyrannical figures like Bush who consider themselves above the law and capable of doing whatever they want even when it comes to torturing other human beings or even their children. Historically speaking it has been big government that has impinged upon the freedoms and liberties of the people. We must remember that Ben Franklin said, "They who would give up an essential liberty for temporary security, deserve neither liberty or security."

"To keep global resource use within prudent limits while the poor raise their living standards, affluent societies need to consume less. Population, consumption, technology, development, and the environment are linked in complex relationships that bear closely on human welfare in the global neighbourhood. Their effective and equitable management calls for a systemic, long-term, global approach guided by the principle of sustainable development, which has been the central lesson from the mounting ecological dangers of recent times. Its universal application is a priority among the tasks of global governance."
United Nations Our Global Neighborhood 1995

-David Dees

The Lies Which Lead To War
October 9, 2006
Zen Garcia

With 72% of U.S. Troops on the ground in Iraq calling for an end to the war this year, and 51% of Americans believing that removing Saddam Hussein from power not worth the number of U.S. Military casualties and the financial cost of the war, when will our government listen to the voice and will of the people? Will they listen to us as they don't seem to be able to hear the Iraqi's themselves, as they have been calling for immediate withdrawal for years. A poll put out by USA Today in 2004 reports: "But while they acknowledge benefits from dumping Saddam a year ago, Iraqis no longer see the presence of the American-led military as a plus. Asked whether they view the U.S.-led coalition as "liberators" or "occupiers," 71% of all respondents say "occupiers." A growing negative attitude toward the Americans is also reflected in two related survey questions: 53% say they would feel less secure without the coalition in Iraq, but 57% say the foreign troops should leave anyway."

It is clear that the American public, our soldiers, and the Iraqi people themselves want an immediate end to the war in Iraq. It is even clear from a New Zogby Poll that the majority of Americans support impeaching Bush for the warrant less and illegal wiretapping being done against American citizens especially now that it is known the administration is targeting groups opposed to the illegal war; and yet the spineless Democrats run anytime anyone like Russ Feingold calls for censuring Bush or John Murtha calls for immediate withdrawal. If America does not impeach this president, everybody in congress will consider themselves as Bush does now above the law. By a margin of 52% to 43%, Americans want Congress to impeach President Bush if he wiretapped American citizens without a judge's approval, which he did.

If Congress won't move to impeach, vote them out of office (must get rid of the paperless easily hacked unreliable voting machines first) and vote someone in who will, someone hungry to represent the will of the people, someone disgusted with the current corruption running amuck in Washington, DC.

The whole world now knows that the Bush administration lied to get public support for the war by first trying to tie Iraq to the atrocities of September 11th, 2001. Once that admonishment was debunked they tried to frighten American by invoking images of 'mushroom clouds on American soil.' Desperate for something, anything to scare the American public into believing that the nuclear threat from Iraq was real and that Iraq had something to do with 9/11, the administration began a systematic and deliberate attempt to distort links between 9/11, Al-Qaeda, and Saddam Hussein, resulting in 69 percent of Americans believing that Saddam Hussein had part in attacking the United States..

Democratic Senators charged that the White House had fanned the mis-perception by mentioning Hussein and the Sept. 11 attacks in ways suggesting a link. Bush, on March 6, 2003, said, "Saddam Hussein is a threat to our nation. September the 11th changed the strategic thinking, at least, as far as I was concerned, for how to protect our country. My job is to protect the American people. It used to be that we could think that you could contain a person like Saddam Hussein, that oceans would protect us from his type of terror.

September the 11th should say to the American people that we're now a battlefield, that weapons of mass destruction in the hands of a terrorist organization could be deployed here at home."

After the 9/11 Commission came out and publicly stated that there was not a relationship between Saddam, 9/11, and Al-Qaeda, Bush said on June 17, 2004, "The reason I keep insisting that there was a relationship between Iraq and Saddam and Al-Qaeda, because there was a relationship between Iraq and Al Qaeda." He continued exaggerating claims and made several more statements like, "After September the 11th, America had to assess every potential threat in a new light. Our nation awakened to an even greater danger, the prospect that terrorists who killed thousands with hijacked airplanes would kill many more with weapons of mass murder. We had to take a hard look at every place where terrorists might get those weapons. And one regime stood out, the dictatorship of Saddam Hussein." - GWB, Wilkes-Barre, Pennsylvania, Oct. 6, 2004.

They continued their policy of deception by then trying to convince America that she was in imminent danger from a nuclear attack from Iraq. Bush said in a speech on Oct. 7, 2002, "Facing clear evidence of peril, we cannot wait for the final proof -- the smoking gun -- that could come in the form of a mushroom cloud."

Rice said, "we don't want the smoking gun to be a mushroom cloud." On NBC's "Meet the Press," Cheney accused Saddam of "moving aggressively to develop nuclear weapons... to add to his stockpile of chemical and biological arms. Increasingly, we believe that the United States may well become the target of those activities." The whole administration had been hard at work instilling fear to scare America into supporting an illicit invasion, while Bush was behind closed doors with Prime Minister Tony Blair of Britain, busily dreaming up ways to provoke Saddam Hussein into attacking allied forces and in that way justify their war. Recently released minutes on White House letterhead and signed by the President, show that during a private two-hour meeting with Blair in the Oval Office on Jan. 31, 2003, Bush revealed to Blair that he was determined to invade Iraq even without a second UN resolution, and even if international arms inspectors failed to find unconventional weapons. He then discussed a proposal to paint a United States surveillance plane in the colors of the United Nations in hopes of drawing fire and setting in motion war. This exact plan was discussed in an earlier 1962 document called Operation Northwoods in which the U.S. Joint Chiefs of Staff drew up and approved clandestine operations intending to stage 'terrorism' in order to create American hostility towards Cuba. On page 13 of the 15 page declassified memo, the Joint Chiefs of Staff discuss, "An aircraft at Eglin AFB would be painted and numbered as an exact duplicate for a civil registered aircraft belonging to a CIA proprietary organization in the Miami area. At a designated time the duplicate would be substituted for the actual civil aircraft and would be loaded with the selected passengers, all boarded under carefully prepared aliases. The actual registered aircraft would be converted to a drone."

On page 8 the Joint Chiefs state, "This plan, incorporating projects selected from the attached suggestions, or from other sources, should be developed to focus all efforts on a specific ultimate objective which would provide adequate justification for US military intervention. Such a plan would enable a logical build-up of incidents to be combined with other seemingly unrelated events to camouflage the ultimate objective and create the necessary impression of Cuban rashness and irresponsibility on a large scale, directed at other countries as well as the United States.

The plan would also properly integrate and time phase the courses of action to be pursued. The desired resultant from the execution of this plan would be to place the United States in the apparent position of suffering defensible grievances from a rash and irresponsible government of Cuba and to develop an inter-national image of a Cuban threat to peace in the Western Hemisphere." Clearly what is being suggested is treasonous actions against our own country by our own military leaders, who also entertain subversive actions against other sovereign nations as a way to make Cuba look bad. Terrorism in the name of anti-communism is still terrorism especially when carried out secretly against the United States by the United States.

Fearing that the window of opportunity to get into Iraq may slip away, the Neo-Con Bush administration set itself on a course to "fix the facts around the policy" as verified by the first leaked Downing Street Minutes. In their rush to war, they blamed intelligence agencies for not gathering together the proper and necessary intelligence needed to assess a proper plan for deciding on whether to go to war or not. However, we know Bush and Blair had already committed themselves to invading Iraq and both ignored any threat assessment that did not support their call for an invasion. America, we had better get serious about reeling in this out of control administration especially now that the very same hawks which premeditatedly lied and deceived the American public into supporting the horror that is now Iraq; are again sounding the drums against Iran, calling for not just conventional but nuclear tactical strikes on over 200 targets in that country.

America please wake up, the lives of children here and all over the world depend on it. We must hold these fear inciting war criminals accountable as it is they themselves who are profiting from the continued violence and occupations of Iraq and Afghanistan through unethical defense investments through the private financial firm, the Carlyle Group. This company is not opened to the public scrutiny or investment, the SEC has never audited them, members consider themselves untouchable much like the privately owned European controlled board directing the Federal Reserve System.

We know that Bush and his whole administration will lie, cheat, and deceive in order to fulfill their Project for a New American Century directive for securing the Middle East through a series of permanent forward staging bases to then be used as preemptive strike capability in securing the fascist interests of the oil corporations dominating government through massive lobbying. How else would these companies secure billion dollar government subsidies at a time of record profit? Why else would the positioning of permanent bases line-up to pipeline plans or drilling agreements?

We must demand accountability. We cannot allow this corrupt administration to purposely lie and deceive the public into supporting bogus wars of aggression against sovereign nations when real threats exist right here at home. There are already myriad reasons to impeach this President as many of his staff and many congressmen are already folding to indictments. So I ask why, why is America not in the streets every day, at the White House and Congress everyday demanding the end of all support for this warmongering, anti-constitutional dictatorial administration.

Our country cannot afford another war anywhere with anybody. We are already drowning in surmounting debts accumulated predominately from the failed war in Iraq and yet regardless, this administration seems hell bent on taking us into further escalations with Iran and Syria. The fact that the U.S. has already warned Turkey of our intent to launch air strikes on Iran and Syria, let's you know how close we are to another full out war as nations will be forced to take sides.

Recently a London Guardian reporter released an article called, "Are we going to war with Iran?" to further investigate allegations of impending war. Seymour Hersh a few days earlier wrote in the New Yorker, that the war against Iran had already begun. "Current and former American military and intelligence officials said that Air Force planning groups are drawing up lists of targets, and teams of American combat troops have been ordered into Iran, under cover, to collect targeting data and to establish contact with anti-government ethnic-minority groups. The officials say that President Bush is determined to deny the Iranian regime the opportunity to begin a pilot program, planned for this spring, to enrich uranium." Colonel Sam Gardner verified Hersh in an interview with Amy Goodman of Democracy Now, "The issue is not whether the Military option would be used but who approved the start of operations already."

Iranian President Mahmoud Ahmadinejad, announced on April 11th that its nuclear engineers had advanced to a new phase in the enrichment of uranium. The Clerics also announced that the nation would speed ahead, in defiance of a United Nations Security Council warning, to produce nuclear fuel on an industrial scale for civil power production as is their right according to the Non-Proliferation Treaty which the US has recently violated by authorizing the production of a new generation of nuclear devices and also by agreeing to sell India nuclear technology when India itself has not signed onto the NPT. America in signing the NPT, promised not to help other countries with their nuclear-weapons technology unless those countries had all their nuclear facilities under international safeguards which India does not and never will. Does this then mean unavoidable war? Are we to wake up one day with our country having attacked Iran? I heard Fox report just a few days ago, that we just may wake up one day and find that our country had already bombed Iran, and that if that were the case it would improve Bush's poll numbers. Does this sound like insanity to anyone else? If you do not wish to see us plunged into further Bush administration chaos, call every one of your federal contacts, Representatives, and Senators right now and bug them continuously without pause, so that they absolutely know, we do not want an attack on Iran and that attacking Iran will only endanger our country and their jobs. Ask them if you really wanted to stop the nuclear program in Iran, why allow the CIA to provide them the blueprints in the first place? If we the U.S. and Britain were really concerned about Iran gathering the necessary program to create a nuclear bomb, why then would our governments allow American and British companies to sell them the exact material needed to advance their nuclear program?

We must ask why British officials would defy their own arms embargo toward Iran, and approve the export of key components necessary to make nuclear weapons? If they were that concerned with a nuclear Iran, why provide the material necessary to advance the nuclear program at all stages? Why wait until they reach the point of activating the technology we've provided for their nuclear programs to cry wolf? President Gerald Ford authorized the Shah to buy and operate a plutonium-extracting and processing facility in 1976, if we were concerned with Iran as a threat, isn't prevention key, meaning never allow them to reach this point?

Scott Ritter a former UN weapons inspector warned us last year of the encroaching war with Iran. The only thing yet to be determined is whether it will be Israel or the US that does the actual air strikes, or whether it will be a joint US-Israeli strike, either way America will be plunged headlong into what will be the catalyst for the next global war. We need to clean house in America, starting with the whole administration but not ending until we've moved through all branches of government destroying the corrupt electronic paperless electoral system and in particular dismantle the lobby system which allows politicians to be bought legally. Remember the people united will never be defeated, the people silenced will never be heard.

> "Our job is to give people not what they want, but what we decide they ought to have."
> Richard Salent, former president, CBS News

-David Dees

The Torture King: Target America
October 29, 2006
Zen Garcia

Government as laid down by our fore fathers, should always support the protection of those rights and liberties established as guiding principles guaranteed to us by the US Constitution and Our Bill of Rights. That is why all public servants sworn to office swear an allegiance and an oath to protect and honor the principles set forth by the US Constitution. Somehow, somewhere along the way that oath has become meaningless as everyday big government attacks and maims the very heart of the articles that laid the foundation to make this nation the great country it had become.

With the passing of the Military Commissions Act of 2006, almost 800 years of international precedence to protect human rights through habeas corpus law was nullified into non-existence and replaced by a new and terrifying expansion of tyrannical Executive rule.

"The president can now, with the approval of Congress, indefinitely hold people without charge, take away protections against horrific abuse, put people on trial based on hearsay evidence, authorize trials that can sentence people to death based on testimony literally beaten out of witnesses, and slam shut the courthouse door for habeas petitions," said ACLU Executive Director Anthony D. Romero.

Fearing the loss of Republican power in the mid-term elections, the inept and overly corrupt GOP congress has now authorized the President to establish special military tribunals to prosecute 'terrorist' suspects accused of threatening National Security. The rules permit the exclusion of a defendant from trial should 'secret' evidence be presented in a case and allows for conviction based on hearsay evidence or coerced statements solicited through torture. This Draconian legislation also authorizes a three-officer military panel the power to determine a detainee's status as an 'enemy combatant' and whether they are qualified for indefinite detention without the right of a habeas corpus petition to challenge the legality of detention in federal constitutional court.

The law also allows the president to ""interpret the meaning and application" of international standards for prisoner treatment meaning that the CIA can continue their secret program of kidnapping, excuse me 'rendition,' interrogating suspects abroad, outsourcing them to territories where the rule of law does not exist, and torture can be used unabated. There is even a war crimes immunity clause to protect interrogators for past actions which the US Supreme Court in June said violated U.S. and international law. Those that had committed such acts could have been prosecuted as war criminals for past behaviors. Interrogators had been refusing to continue the program as implemented prior to the passing of this law, but now it's business as usual with even greater move toward instituting new techniques as this law also narrows the range of activities that constitute a violation of Common Article 3 of the Geneva Conventions which outlaws torture, cruel, and inhumane treatment by international standards.

The most heinous aspect of this Draconian legislation is that it expands the definition of what a detainee is to include US citizens labeled 'enemy combatants' or 'domestic terrorists' by Section 802 of the first USA Patriot act which states, "domestic terrorism means activities that-- `(A) involve acts dangerous to human life that are a violation of the criminal laws of the United States or of any State; `(B) appear to be intended-- (i) to intimidate or coerce a civilian population; (ii) to influence the policy of a government by intimidation or coercion; or (iii) to affect the conduct of a government by mass destruction, assassination, or kidnapping; and (C) occur primarily within the territorial jurisdiction of the United States .'

Anyone who offers "material support" to someone engaged in hostilities against the US can be held indefinitely in military detention, regardless of whether he or she actually engaged in hostilities, and can be forced to relinquish

"citizenship by serving in a hostile terrorist organization. Specifically, an American could be expatriated if, with the intent to relinquish nationality, he becomes a member of, or provides material support to, a group that the United States has designated as a 'terrorist organization,' if that group is engaged in hostilities against the United States."

Taken into account with the broader definition of Section 501 of the Domestic Security Enhancement Act of 2003 or Patriot Act II, any violation of Federal or State law can result in the "enemy combatant" terrorist designation which means that regardless of being an American citizen if designated as an 'enemy combatant,' one can be denied habeas corpus, held indefinitely, tortured, convicted, and even sentenced to death based on traditionally non-admissible hearsay or coerced testimony, and possibly summarily executed with secret state evidence which never has to be released to public scrutiny. "The establishment of the writ of habeas corpus ... are perhaps greater securities to liberty and republicanism than any it [the Constitution] contains. ...[T]he practice of arbitrary imprisonments have been, in all ages, the favorite and most formidable instruments of tyranny. - Alexander Hamilton

"What does that mean for the American people? It means the same thing it did for Jose Padilla. You'll recall that Padilla was arrested in Chicago for terrorism and transferred to military custody, where, according to Padilla, he was tortured and involuntarily injected with drugs. The government's position is that since the entire world is a battlefield in which the war on terrorism is being waged, U.S. officials now have the power to arrest any American suspected of terrorism, place him in military custody, and subject him to the same "unlawful enemy combatant" treatment that Padilla received, until the war on terrorism has finally been won, no matter how long that takes."

Cheney said the war on terror will not end in our lifetimes. He also said in a Sept 16, 2001 interview with Tim Russert of Meet The Press, "We also have to work, though, sort of the dark side, if you will. We've got to spend time in the shadows in the intelligence world. A lot of what needs to be done here will have to be done quietly, without any discussion, using sources and methods that are available to our intelligence agencies, if we're going to be successful. That's the world these folks operate in, and so it's going to be vital for us to use any means at our disposal, basically, to achieve our objective." Cheney seems to have known that torture would be used to extract information from people considered terrorists. They are trying to rationalize that America needs to be able to torture 'terrorists' to protect the people. In an interview Tuesday with WDAY of Fargo, North Dakota, Cheney was asked if "a dunk in water is a no-brainer if it can save lives." The vice president replied, "Well, it's a no-brainer for me, but for a while there I was criticized as being the vice president for torture. We don't torture. That's not what we're involved in." The people, however, are worried about the indiscriminate torture of everybody including American citizens.

One has to remember that according to Patriot Act I, an 'enemy combatant' is anyone who engages in expressing dissenting view or opinion against government policy when not satisfied with current policy. Under the Military Commissions Act of 2006, any person deemed an 'enemy combatant' whether an American citizen or not, can be tortured, detained, and denied Constitutional protections should the Executive branch consider that person a threat.

Jacob Hornberger wrote, "The only reason that Americans do not find themselves at Gitmo is because the Pentagon, in its discretion, decided not to send Americans suspected of terrorism to Gitmo. That discretionary decision could be changed at any time, just as the current policy of "rendering" foreigners to Syria and other tyrannical regimes for torture can be changed at any time to include Americans.

The same holds true for Americans accused of terrorism in the future - they could easily find themselves before a kangaroo military tribunal fighting for their lives rather than in a U.S. district court. After all, no one should forget the Padilla doctrine. Even though Jose Padilla, an American citizen, is in federal court now, the president and the Pentagon have made it perfectly clear that they now have the power to arrest any American for terrorism and send him to the military for punishment, bypassing the federal-court system. In fact, there's little doubt that if Padilla is acquitted in federal court, the feds intend to yank him back into military custody as an "enemy combatant" in the "war on terrorism," despite the bar on double jeopardy in the Bill of Rights."

"The provisions of Bush's new torture law mean that Americans have lost the key, constitutional right on which Anglo-American criminal law (and criminal-law procedures in true democracies in general) is founded; that's the basic right of an individual to know why he or she is being apprehended and detained. Now, technically, as in Stalin's Soviet Union, Hitler's Germany, Mao's China or Pol Pot's Cambodia, anyone labeled an "enemy combatant" - again, by whom; by Bush? - can be whisked away and never heard from again. That kind of authority, in the hands of corrupt or untruthful politicians, may or may not be an effective tool in some kind of "war on terror," but it certainly can be a useful tool when it comes to silencing their opponents." said Edward M. Gomez, a former U.S. diplomat and staff reporter at TIME.

There is a case pending right now where an Iraqi born American citizen, Mohammed Munaf, is in the fight of his life against the Iraqi and US governments for alleged involvement in a conspiracy to abduct and hold hostage for two months three Romanian journalists in Iraq. He was sentenced to death just last week and is being held in a US-run prison at the Baghdad airport. Munaf, arrested by US troops last year, was charged with kidnapping three Romanian journalists and holding them hostage for nearly two months. "Just weeks ago, it appeared he would be set free. Munaf's attorneys claim the presiding judge promised to dismiss the charges after he concluded there was no material evidence to support a conviction."The presiding judge had been prepared to dismiss charges until two US military officials including an unnamed general stepped into the courtroom and requested a private meeting with the judge. The defense was asked to leave the courtroom. One officer claiming to be an official from the Romanian embassy said Romania "demanded" Munaf be put to death. 15 minutes later the judge called in the defense, ruled Munaf guilty, and then sentenced he and four other defendants to death without hearing any additional evidence.

In an emergency motion filed two weeks ago, Munaf's attorneys wrote, "Mr. Munaf was convicted and sentenced to death by an Iraqi court operating under glaring procedural deficiencies and the direct manipulation of US military personnel." One of the 3 victims Edward Ovidiu Ohanesian, whom traveled to Iraq with Munaf to interview former interim Prime Minister Ayad Allawi, said he finds it difficult to believe that Munaf was involved in the kidnapping as he himself endured the same ordeal as the other 3 kidnapped victims. "I think he was a collateral victim," he said in an interview with the Associated Press. "Munaf was held with us the entire time." Ohanesian said. Reporters Without Borders said it was outraged that Munaf was charged with the kidnapping of three Romanian journalists. "We have confidence that the Romanian justice system will do its utmost to shed light on this disturbing case. They must punish all those implicated in what appears to be a put up job, in line with their wrongdoing".

When questioned, representatives of the Romanian government said that they had not authorized any US official to speak on its behalf, was not in fact seeking the death penalty in this case, and did not want to push ahead with charges against Munaf because of a lack of evidence. Lawyers representing Munaf stateside last week filed a petition in federal court to stop the transfer of Munaf from American to Iraqi custody where the sentence would be carried out; citing that "his conviction in the Iraqi court is a farce and that he was not allowed to present evidence or witnesses in his defense and that Munaf made incriminating statements only after threats of violence and sexual assault (were levied) against him and his family." That petition was rejected by a federal judge just three days ago and Munaf will now be handed over to Iraqi authorities where he will be executed. In declaring the fight on the war on terror, the Bush administration has consolidated presidential power, reduced civil liberties, ramped up government secrecy, and granted themselves and their agents, Draconian police state measures which decimate the US Constitution and our Bill of Rights.

With the passing of the Military Commissions Act, the Executive branch effectively eliminates Habeas Corpus for anyone considered an 'enemy combatant' anywhere in the world and establishes a separate judiciary in which to enact punishment which may include sole authority, power to detain, torture, indefinitely hold, and even execute anyone the President so wishes. He has stripped the right of the judiciary to review cases the Executive brings against 'enemy combatants.'

Jakob Kellenberger, the president of the International Committee of the Red Cross, criticized the government's passing of the new U.S. Military Commissions Act because it has weakened protections guaranteed by the Geneva Conventions by broadening the definition of an enemy combatant, failing to guarantee prisoners the right to a fair trial and by failing to explicitly prohibit the use of evidence obtained by coercive torture. The International Committee of the Red Cross also issued its second ever "concern" regarding the actions of a warring Nation. The first "concern" issued by the ICRC came in 1944 with concern over Nazi Germany's treatment of concentration camp detainees. In part 3 of this series I will compare legislation and tactics used by Nazi Germany to legislation and tactics used by the Bush administration, as it seems we are following the very same blue print. "Those who forget the lessons of history are doomed to repeat it." God help us all.

"There does exist and has existed for a generation, an international . . . network which operates, to some extent, in the way the radical right believes the Communists act. In fact, this network, which we may identify as the Round Table Groups, has no aversion to cooperating with the Communists, or any other groups and frequently does so. I know of the operations of this network because I have studied it for twenty years and was permitted for two years, in the early 1960s, to examine its papers and secret records. I have no aversion to it or to most of its aims and have, for much of my life, been close to it and to many of its instruments. I have objected, both in the past and recently, to a few of its policies . . . but in general my chief difference of opinion is that it wishes to remain unknown, and I believe its role in history is significant enough to be known."
-Professor Carroll Quigley, Tragedy and Hope, 1966.

-David Dees

Kissing Cousins, Staged Elections, and The False Left-Right Paradigm
November 4, 2006
Zen Garcia

We are quickly approaching another midterm election year wherein active voters will head to the polls and wonder whether they still have the power to affect a positive change into American reality. The odds are stacked against us, simply because the GOP owns, controls, and distribute the no paper-unverifiable easily manipulated electronic voting machines, we use to determine elections. If you believe in our one vote one person electoral system then you absolutely must demand that the election system be made review able and accountable with a paper trail for voter verification. We are in danger of losing all hope if we do not step up soon to change the direction of this country. America is losing her allies one by one as world opinion shifts. We must get the Decider-in-Chief lackeys out of office this election cycle as this may well be our last chance to remove some of the Neo-con Hawks bent on furthering escalations in the Middle East into what would be the third Crusader war, a battle for world dominance and the control of the last remaining resources of the planet. America realizes now that the Bush administration is trying to lead America down the road of global conquest and eventual control of the world as stated in their Project for the New American Century document called "Rebuilding America's Defenses"; if we continue to go the PNAC way, we will find our country immersed in multiple wars and too weak to offset those who really mean us harm. This document spells out their plan clearly - 9/11 was their spark, their call for a new Pearl Harbor to instigate this plan of global dominance and perpetual war. Written in 2000, they noted that "the process of transformation, even if it brings revolutionary change, is likely to be a long one, absent some catastrophic and catalyzing event -- like a new Pearl Harbor."

Even Lou Dobbs from CNN, propaganda central, knows Bush cares nothing for America and has reported numerously on how Bush and globalist friends desire to bring us into a North American Union by surrendering America's national sovereignty. It doesn't matter whether you believe Bush is a globalist who supports the New World Order, one world government or not, the fact is that we are being forced into a Pan-American Union. So what to do to stop the globalists bent on destroying America? The real question remains - Who do we vote into Congress here in this country, that could bring down the Bush House of cards and affect true and positive change for all of the citizens of this nation, and maybe restore our connections, good will with the rest of the world? This is the greatest dilemma facing American voters, besides the no-paper-trail-easily rigged electronic voting machines.

Who can we trust? We can't trust the Republicans. They are proving themselves to be nothing more than Bush Administration lapdogs, willing to pass any piece of legislation, no matter how corrupt and offensive, just to hold the party line. We can't trust the Democrats either, as they are nothing more than spineless, indecisive suck-ups that can't even work together to oppose the greatest threat to our fragile democracy, George W. Bush. Outside of Russ Feingold and maybe a few others, Democrats aren't even doing the job they ran for, namely upholding congressional powers to maintain the checks and balances intended by our founding fathers when they established a government of 3 equal branches necessary to preserve the Republic. Nancy Pelosi, who would be Speaker of the House if Democrats take over in November, all but ruled out launching impeachment hearings against President Bush, citing on NBC's "Meet the Press" hosted by Tim Russert: "Democrats are not about impeachment - Democrats are about bringing the country together." Asked about Conyers' repeated calls for an impeachment investigation, Pelosi said, "I am the leader. Our caucus will decide where we're going," she declared. "I don't see us going to a place of impeachment."

Since the Republicans and the Democrats obviously can't or are unwilling to do their jobs, what shall we do when it is clear that Bush considers himself above the law as Commander-in-Chief and the maybe soon Speaker of the House Democratic leader, Nancy Pelosi won't do her job to investigate the corruption of the current GOP Congress? With both parties having failed us, where do we as a nation wanting to end the war in Iraq and avoid a war with Iran, place our vote when both the Democrats and the Republicans are pro-the never ending war on terror and pro-stay the course?

We should use this opportunity as a nation to vote in Independents, giving power to a 3rd party which both the Democrats and Republicans then would have to work with to get legislation passed. We don't have to control either of the larger parties; we just have to give enough control to 3rd parties to be able to swing the votes of either party. Voting Independents into power that - 1.) truly wish to represent the wishes of the people 2.) will stand up in truth and sincerity against the injustice of the preemption policy and illegal wars 3.) will go the full measure to impeach Bush and company, and 4.) has no lobby ties and is in no way controlled by corporations or the rich; we may just be able to take back this country from the Neo-Cons who hijacked the elections of 2000 and 2004.

In this way the will of the people will be injected back into the legislative process and perhaps the people can again have a voice and a way to restore integrity to Congress, affecting a positive change for the whole world. The closely watched Connecticut Senatorial race is a sign of how America feels about the Bush Administration, run-away Republican corruption, and Incumbent Democratic support for White House policies. It is clear that America is ready to clean house in the political arena. We realize our nation and security are in trouble because of the incompetence of the Bush presidency. He has made over 750 different signing statements declaring his authority to ignore any law he chooses and to interpret it any way he wants. With his careless disregard for our own Constitution and Bill of Rights, the American people are everyday waking up more and more into what anyone would recognize as a Fascist police state, where laws are decided and declared by those who consider themselves above the reach of the laws they make.

Unless you know that the past 2 Presidential elections have already been hijacked and that it is likely that the next presidential election and even these mid-term elections probably will too, you will feel powerless in using your voting privilege to challenge the obviously corrupt way elections are being handled. We must at least vote to know that our vote doesn't matter so that in knowing it doesn't matter, we as the people realize what must be done to correct the deficiencies. Another powerful force that the average American must contest is the lobby system in Washington. Powerful lobby groups are used to giving gifts to politicians who being used to receiving them always seem to posture themselves to implement the wishes of lobbying ties. With the Abramoff scandal unraveling in a federal court in Washington, now is the perfect time to demand lobbying reform. We cannot compete against big business interests which has hundreds of full-time lobbyist to court each member of Congress, White House, and all other governmental agencies.

Now I will make you aware of how phony the left-right, Democratic-Republican, 2 party system which has dominated American politics for 200 hundred years is. "The so-called Left-Right political spectrum is our creation. In fact, it is accurately reflects our careful, artificial polarization of the population on phony issues that prevents the issue of our power from arising in their minds... We control the Right-Left conflict such that both forms of liberty are suppressed to the degree we require. Our own liberty rests not on legal or 'moral' rights," but on our own control of the government bureaucracy and courts which apply the complex, subjective regulations we dupe the public into supporting for our benefit." - The Occult Technology of Power

To prove the point I just made, take into account the 2004 election between Kerry and Bush. Do you know that Bush and Kerry are cousins of Hugh Hefner. Ancestry.com reveals that Bush and Kerry are not only related to Prince Charles, but have a common ancestor, Vlad the Impaler, the real Count Dracula. With that in mind is it even slightly odd that both have sworn blood oaths of loyalty to secret societies (Yale Skull & Bones) which have the destruction of America's national sovereignty for a New World Order one world government controlled by a United Nations Peace Keeping force as their driving motivation. Is it any wonder looking back now that Kerry came out and conceded to his cousin Bush just to stop the recount in Ohio even though he would have easily won the race.

The secret society which owns the allegiance of Bush and Kerry, also owns the allegiance of many of the nation's most powerful men and families. Skull and Bones secretly "taps" fifteen juniors each year, by seniors to head the next year's group. The family names of Skull & Bones roll off the tongue like an elite party list - Lord, Whitney, Taft, Jay, Bundy, Harriman, Weyerhaeuser, Pinchot, Rockefeller, Goodyear, Sloane, Stimson, Phelps, Perkins, Pillsbury, Kellogg, Vanderbilt, Bush, Lovett and on. For a roster of Skull and Bones members go here.

Bruce and Kristine Harrison, Hawaii-based publishers of historical databases traced back the family histories of Bush and Democratic Sen. John Kerry. They found out Kerry and Bush are exactly 16th cousins, three times removed. Playboy founder Hugh Hefner is the president's ninth cousin, twice removed. Both the president and the Massachusetts Senator can claim ties to figures ranging from Charlemagne to Walt Disney to Marilyn Monroe, Harrison said. In his book, "Bush Kerry and Their Other Cousins," Alexander Books explores his own family tree to show how George W. Bush, John Kerry, Dick Cheney, and Senator Johnny "John" Reid Edwards are all related to most of the Presidents of the United States. Think this is the first time cousins have run against each other for the Presidency? Just as in 2004, the elites hijacked the elections in 2000 and had Gore concede the Presidency to his royal cousin George 'the decider' Bush. 2004 was a repeat of 2000 except that it was a different cousin conceding to Bush. Check this link to see how Gore and Bush relate to each other ancestrally.

Burke's Peerage, a revered guide to the breeding of the aristocracy, said both Bush and his rival Al Gore are of royal descent, but investigations deep into their heritage show Bush has far more noble and royal connections. Bush is closely related to every European monarch on and off the throne -- including the King of Albania -- and has kinship with every member of Britain's royal family, the

House of Windsor. He is a 13th cousin of Britain's Queen Mother, and of her daughter Queen Elizabeth and is a 13th cousin once removed of the heir to the throne, Prince Charles. Documented as far back as the early 15th century, He has a direct descent from Henry III and from Henry VIII's sister Mary Tudor, who was also the wife of Louis XI of France. He is also descended from Charles II of England.

"It is now clear that Mr. Gore and Mr. Bush have an unusually large number of royal and noble descents," said Harold Brooks-Baker, publishing director of Burke's Peerage. "In point of fact, never in the history of the United States have two presidential candidates been as well endowed with royal alliances. There had always been a significant "royalty factor" in those who aspired to the White House, with Presidents George Washington, Thomas Jefferson, Franklin and Theodore Roosevelt and Ronald Reagan, among others, all boasting blue blood links." Democrat candidate Al Gore, has a somewhat less illustrious gene pool though he too is a cousin by relation to Bush. "Being a descendant of Edward I, he is also a cousin of former U.S. president Richard Nixon, who resigned from the White House in 1974 for his part in the Watergate scandal." Gore also has direct links to the holy Roman Empire. He is a descendant of Roman Emperors Louis II, Charles II and Louis I and is therefore also a direct descendant of Charlemagne -- the eight-century Emperor.

Yes, the real shocker is that the election system is nothing more than staged theatrics. Researchers now know that 43 men who were Presidents of the U.S.A. are related, and that 33 of those Presidents can be traced back to the bloodline of Charlemagne, who in the year 800 was crowned by Pope Leo III to be Holy Roman Emperor, the first head of an empire that would last over 1000 years! 26 of the 42 Presidents are cousins to the seventh degree at most. David Icke verifies this research in his book "The Biggest Secret." Are the alarms going off in your head? Democratic and Republican candidates are "chosen" by the "Elitist" super rich who have throughout history claimed the 'divine right' to rule.

"The Right has such a fear of the Left's democratic collectivism and the Left such a hatred for what is it sees as the Right's elitist, rugged individualism that there is little danger that they will ever join forces to overturn our government-backed monopolies even though we violate the ideals of both left and right." - The Occult Technology of

Power The American royalty are also tied to the other ruling families of the world in what is a New World Order familial conspiracy, perpetuated by wealthy elites having centralized wealth and power by intermarrying among themselves and not ever allowing 'outsiders' to be privy to their efforts. This powerful group of ruling elites is known to the world as the Bildeberger group. So if this is true what do we do to take back America? The first thing to do is to educate yourself and then educate others. This is not a time to be silent or shocked into submission. The ruling elite are pushing faster and harder to implement their New World Order, one world government prophesied in Revelations.

Albert Pike sent a letter to Giuseppe Mazzini about the need to create three global wars in order to implement a one world order in which world government could be controlled through the United Nations. Recently, the UN called for its own standing army, and the ability to declare global taxes. It is only a matter of time before they control the might to enforce that tax upon the peoples of the world. The 3rd World War is looming. We can avoid it if you know your enemy and their agenda. We must understand where we are to understand where we are going. Know that most career politicians have been compromised and are controlled no matter whether their Democrat or Republican. The best thing to do to take back our government is for common people to run for office yourself, in the very least vote for Independents or new representatives. We must vote out career Incumbents as most have already been compromised and are supporting the globalist agenda. This may very well be our last chance to use our power to redirect the focus and policies of our country.

"The world is governed by very different personages from what is imagined by those who are not behind the scenes." Benjamin Disraeli, British Prime Minister. 1876.

"No one will enter the New World Order unless he or she will make a pledge to worship Lucifer. No one will enter the New Age unless he will take a Luciferian Initiation."

David Spangler, Director of Planetary Initiative, United Nations

-David Dees

The Decider's Plan to Provoke War with Iran
January 31, 2007
Zen Garcia

Why an escalation and why now when tens of thousands, up to half a million Americans have taken to the streets to of Washington, DC to implore congress that you cannot oppose the war and still fund it. The citizenry has made it clear that we absolutely do not support Bush's immoral illegal war against Iraq and failed foreign policy in fighting the war o terror. Bush cannot even claim that he has made the American people safer especially since the borders were and are still wide open, our ports are not secure, and his administration failed even to implement the 9-11 commission recommendations for protecting the country.

The BBC released a poll on Jan 23rd, 2007 which clearly shows that the view of the US's role in the world has deteriorated both internationally and domestically. When asked about US military presence in the Middle East, an average of 68% of respondents across 25 countries including the US, answered that our country "provokes more conflict than it prevents". Now that the rubber stamp Republican controlled Senate has been dethroned, members of the President's own party have expressed public concern over the Decider's planned escalation of the war, the real question remains - Why a troop escalation or 'surge' and why now? Is it really to stabilize Baghdad and ease the sectarian violence or does the Decider have something even more sinister in mind like provoking a Greater Middle East War with planned conventional and even nuclear air strikes against Iran's nuclear power infrastructure?

Retired USAF Colonel Sam Gardiner wrote an article entitled, The Pieces Are Being Put in Place, released January 13th, 2007 "The pieces are moving. They'll be in place by the end of February. The United States will be able to escalate military operations against Iran. The White House keeps saying there are no plans to attack Iran. Obviously, the facts suggest otherwise. Equally as clear, the Iranians will read what the Administrations is doing not what it is saying. It is possible the White House strategy is just implementing a strategy to put pressure on Iran on a number of fronts, and this will never amount to anything. On the other hand, if the White House is on a path to strike Iran, we'll see a few more steps unfold."

What are some of those steps? We already have a few clear signs that the United States is provoking dissent and supporting opposition groups in Iran, Syria, and Lebanon, not to mention that our second carrier group has moved into the Persian Gulf something that has not happened since the invasion of Iraq in 2003. On January 25, 2007, Israeli Prime Minister, Ehud Olmert, gave clear warning that his country was prepared to use military force to prevent Tehran from obtaining a nuclear weapon. "Israeli military officials warned this week that Israel - acting alone or in coordination with the US - could launch preemptive military strikes against Iran before the end of this year."

On Jan 15th, Michael Roston released an article about a leaked Jan. 9th memo from the banking division of ING Group entitled "Attacking Iran: The market impact of a surprise Israeli strike on its nuclear facilities." The ING memo was first sent to Raw Story as an anonymous tip and confirmed by staff at the bank's emerging markets office. The full PDF documents can be downloaded at this link for the Jan. 9 report, and this link for the Jan. 15 update. The bank sees February or March as a timeline for an Israeli or US strike on Iran. They were warning their investors that should such an attack take place it could be catastrophic for the world. "Geopolitical tensions will likely rise in February/March, impacting on risk appetite and asset prices across the board."

Whether it's Israel or the United States that actually does the initial bombing, the fact is any strikes against Iran whether conventional or nuclear in capability only promises to destabilize the fragile world order even further and force the entire world to unite against the pre-emptive strike doctrine of the United States as outlined by the Project for a New American Century's document "Rebuilding America's Defenses." The Neo-Conservatives currently running this country and still in power, believe "The United States is the world's only superpower, combining preeminent military power, global technological leadership, and the world's largest economy. Moreover, America stands at the head of a system of alliances which includes the world's other leading democratic powers. At present the United States faces no global rival. America's grand strategy should aim to preserve and extend this advantageous position as far into the future as possible."

General Leonid Ivashov, once chief of the Military cooperation department at the Russian federation's Ministry of defense and Joint chief of staff of the Russian armies, and current vice-president of the Academy on geopolitical affairs; wrote in a article called "Iran Must Get Ready to Repel a Nuclear Attack" dated Jan 24th, 2007, in which he said, "The war in Iraq was just one element in a series of steps in the process of regional destabilization. It was only a phase in the process of getting closer to dealing with Iran and other countries, which the US declared or will declare rouge. However it is not easy for the US to get involved in yet another military campaign while Iraq and Afghanistan are not "pacified" (the US lacks the resources necessary for the operation). Besides, protests against the politics of the Washington Neo-cons intensify all over the world." He goes on to say that, "Some people tend to believe that concerns over the world's protests can stop the US. I don't think so.

The importance of this factor should not be overstated. In the past, I have spent hours talking to Milosevic, trying to convince him that NATO was preparing to attack Yugoslavia. For a long time, he could not believe this and kept telling me: 'Just read the UN Charter. What grounds will they have to do it?' But they did it. They ignored the international law outrageously and did it. What do we have now? Yes, there was a shock, there was indignation. But the result is exactly what the aggressors wanted - Milosevic is dead, Yugoslavia is partitioned, and Serbia is colonized - NATO officers have set up their headquarters in the country's ministry of defense. The same things happened to Iraq. There were a shock and indignation. But what matters to the Americans is not how big the shock is, but how high are the revenues of their military-industrial complex." General Ivashov warned the World Economic Forum in Davos, Switzerland, last week that he expects the US to strike Iran by the end of April.

Recently (Jan 13) the Bush administration ordered a raid on an Iranian office in Irbil and detained five people to investigate whether they were involved in "illegal or terrorist" activity. More recently (Jan 23rd) Bush authorized U.S. forces in Iraq to take "whatever actions are necessary to counter Iranian agents deemed a threat to American troops or the Iraqi public." Think the Decider is trying to provoke Iran into attacking US forces so that he will have the pre-text to broaden the war with Iran? The same thing happened in the lead up to the invasion in Iraq. The bombing campaign against Iraq began long before the start of the official war. The US had pretty much wiped out all radar facilities and air defenses before the official invasion. Bush was hoping that Saddam Hussein would retaliate so that he would have an 'easier' time justifying his war. Because Saddam would not retaliate, Bush was forced into making up lies to conjure public support for the war.

On Jan. 22nd, an article appeared in the Dubai paper called the Gulf News entitled "Is Bush planning war against Iran?" which opened with "It is now clear that the US President George W. Bush has decided to confront Iran - politically, economically and militarily - rather than engage it in negotiations, as he was advised to do by James

Baker and Lee Hamilton in their Iraq Study Group report." The Guardian of London just released an article called, "Iran Warned As Troop Surge Begins." The article confirms the Gulf News article as stated, "The Bush administration rejected calls last month by the bipartisan Iraq Study Group led by the former secretary of state, James Baker, to open dialogue with Iran and has opted instead for a new confrontational approach."

The mainstream news in all parts of the world outside of the US has been widely reporting that many intelligence services from many countries believe that the White House plans to strike Iran before Bush and Cheney lose power and leave office in 2008, and before Blair leaves office in April of 2007. In fact, the World Economic Forum opened January 24 with discussion and a warning from the Secretary General of the League of Arab States Amr Moussa, "There is a 50/50 chance the United States will attack Iran and any such strike would risk spreading sectarian violence through the Middle East... we hope that it won't happen. Attacking Iran would be counterproductive." Moussa also said - the United States needs to move from use of military force towards dialogue, both to resolve the violence in Iraq and to reduce U.S.-Iranian tensions. He added that he favoured proposals for talks with Iran and Syria. "If there were to be a war, other genies will get out of the bottle. You cannot imagine the impact on the Gulf countries, on the Mediterranean."

Paul Craig Roberts, Assistant Secretary of the Treasury in the Reagan administration, wrote an article called - Bush Is About To Attack Iran - Why Can't Americans See It? "...bankers and businessmen from such US allies as Bahrain and the United Arab Emirates all warned of the coming attack and its catastrophic consequences for the Middle East and the world... Rather than winding down one war, Bush is starting another. The entire world knows this and is discussing Bush's planned attack on Iran in many forums. It is only Americans who haven't caught on. A few senators have said that Bush must not attack Iran without the approval of Congress, and postings on the Internet demonstrate worldwide awareness that Iran is in the Bush Regime's cross hairs. But Congress and the Media--and the demonstration in Washington--are focused on Iraq."

If you still don't believe that the US or Israel will attack Iran, please check out William Thomas' story released Ja 25th, 2007 called

"Wrestling With The Devil Behind The Story Of Israel's Aborted Nuclear Strike." Thomas asserts in his article that Israel as recently as Jan. 7th attempted to send fighters into Iran to bomb the its nuclear facilities. The bombing did not take place because US fighters intercepted them enroute over Iraq and forced them to turn back without their payload delivery. "According to this very reliable source, on two previous occasions Israeli fighter-bombers armed with nuclear bombs have headed "downtown" before being turned back over Iraq. The January 7th mission, which trespassed beyond 160 station before being recalled by Israeli authorities, comprised three IAF F-16s. Each carried conventional munitions - as well as a single 20-kiloton nuclear bomb. The atomic detonation that razed the city of Hiroshima and killed 140,000 people outright was a 13-kiloton blast. [Agence France-Presse Aug 6/05]"

We are living in very serious times. The American public is being kept in the dark so that the Decider can get away with enflaming World War III which started after the staged attack of September 11th, 2001. Call your Congress people and tell them to force the President to stop his insane pursuit to 'escalate' war with Iran. The troop surge is about provoking and preparing war with Iran and has nothing to do with stabilizing Iraq. The plan is to escalate tension further so sectarian violence divides the Middle East along ethnic lines. It has always been divide and rule. Wake up people and take America back for our children and our children's' children. We are running out of time but time enough remains for us to act.

> "A really efficient totalitarian state would be one in which the all-powerful executive of political bosses and their army of managers control a population of slaves who do not have to be coerced, because they love their servitude. To make them love it is the task assigned, in present-day totalitarian states, to ministries of propaganda, newspaper editors and schoolteachers.... The greatest triumphs of propaganda have been accomplished, not by doing something, but by refraining from doing. Great is truth, but still greater, from a practical point of view, is silence about truth."
>
> - Aldous Huxley Brave New World

-David Dees

Fallen Heroes: The Return to Civilian Disability
February 14, 2007
Zen Garcia

America loves her heroes, cherishes her soldiers' honor and sacrifices they've made for country and nation. We salute the colors of our flag in unison song, to uphold the memory of all those veterans who have put their all on line risking life, limb, and family to insure our freedoms' and collective liberty. We mark passing holidays to celebrate their commitment to duty and our traditional way of life.

Those that have died in battle fighting to protect our people have been memorialized in tribute. Monuments stand tall in our nation's capitol as a reminder of the sacrifices they've made for us all. A whole generation of wounded soldiers are returning home from war; some mangled beyond recognition, some burnt, some limbless some like myself with life-long spinal cord injury, others with traumatic brain injuries, many with post traumatic stress disorders which may forever haunt them with nightmarish dreams. Recovery will be picking up pieces of themselves, trying to make sense of the jigsaw puzzle that is now their shattered life, surrendered to the cause of the Decider's immoral war, a war the Cheney Energy Task Force said was necessary to preserve our national security.

When first injured I spent my fair share of wide eyed nights trying to make sense of circumstance, conjuring up ghosts of my former life, lovers of my former self. Like me they'll think about what was, before insane circumstance when they lived 'normally' like all other people, desiring nothing more than the peace and prosperity that had been the American dream. The people want peace and desire it for all others, but certain aspects of government want war and will lie to begin it and cheat to sustain it.

Before Dwight D. Eisenhower left the limelight of public service, he made it a point to warn our country about the dangers of the military industrial complex. He said, "We now stand ten years past the midpoint of a century that has witnessed four major wars among great nations. Three of these involved our own country. Despite these holocausts America is today the strongest, the most influential and most productive nation in the world. Understandably proud of this pre-eminence, we yet realize that America's leadership and prestige depend, not merely upon our unmatched material progress, riches and military strength, but on how we use our power in the interests of world peace and human betterment..."

Fearing a permanent war driven economy he continued, "We annually spend on military security more than the net income of all United State corporations. This conjunction of an immense military establishment and a large arms industry is new in the American experience. The total influence-economic, political, even spiritual-is felt in every city, every state house, every office of the Federal government. We recognize the imperative need for this development. Yet we must not fail to comprehend its grave implications. Our toil, resources and livelihood are all involved; so is the very structure of our society. In the councils of government, we must guard against the acquisition of unwarranted influence, whether sought or unsought, by the military-industrial complex. The potential for the disastrous rise of misplaced power exists and will persist."

Obviously, we as a nation did not heed his warning and so war rules the day. Soldiers and civilians are dying in droves everyday leaving behind families irredeemably altered. Young men and women lie in beds even now, recovering in distant lands trying to gather together what's left of the unbroken as they ponder tomorrow's recourse and what the future will bring. Many soldiers joined the military as a result of how they felt when our nation came under attack that fateful day when the Twin Towers were exploded right in front of each one of us, forcing world to witness what is the greatest crime every perpetrated upon the American people. Too many questions remain unanswered of that day for a whole 'war on terror' to be based on and yet the men and women of this nation rose up to protect and pursue who they thought were our enemies. They had determined to take a patriotic stance in defense of our nation, to do something that might protect their families and the lives of their children.

Some had joined the military as a way to escape mediocre jobs, a desperate economy, and lives of restless frustration with friends, who like them, had no sense of optimism for what the future may hold. Many lean on the military to discipline themselves, access adventure while at the same time invest in later education as follow-up to a military career. Some joined as military reserves thinking limited service a great way of supplementing income without necessarily having to devote all of oneself to full time military service. And so many thousands of our nation's brightest and best joined at a time when they knew our nation was to go to war. This would be their way of honoring those who had in other times before stood up in defense of our nation. Since 2001, the U.S. has deployed more than 1 million troops to Iraq and Afghanistan, many have returned with lives affected in such a way that they are unable to go on to other things. And as the Decider seeks hundreds of billions more for war in 2007 consider these facts:

One in three homeless American men are military vets, and that figure is compounding. One in four vets with PTSD who sought medical care from the VA, regularly experienced a two to three month wait just to see a doctor as the ratio of doctors to patients is one doctor for every 500 patients. Over 53,000 soldiers are permanently wounded to the point that they cannot resume active duty. Veteran males aged 20 to 24 have twice the unemployment rate as the national average. There's a 70% divorce rate for returning soldiers.

40% of troops currently being rotated are National Guard or reservists. More than 210,000 of 330,000 the National Guards' reservists have served in Iraq and Afghanistan with mobilizations averaging around 460 days. Nearly a third of active-duty troops, 341,000 men and women, have served two or more overseas tours with 95% of them experiencing problems just getting their pay. Many that may be unfit to serve are being sent back to the front lines on potent anti-depressants, anti-anxiety drugs with little or no counseling, supervision or screening. Over 200 have committed suicide. And at a time when there are more veterans than ever before, the Republican GOP dropped $65 billion in benefits over the next five years beginning 2007. Our soldiers joined the military to protect and defend our nation it is unconscionable that these cuts be administered now while we are still at war. We must support them especially now that so many find themselves critically injured, facing futures of lifelong disabilities.

You would think that the President and our congress would find it a priority to take care of those who give totally of themselves to defend our freedoms. Rep. Jan Schakowsky, a Democrat from Illinois' 9th Congressional District said, "I find it incomprehensible that a plan to reduce benefits for veterans in Illinois and across the country would even be contemplated at a time when hundreds of thousands of active-duty soldiers are risking their lives in Iraq. I join the Disabled American Veterans in asking, Is there is no honor left in the hallowed halls of our government that you choose to dishonor the sacrifices of our nation's heroes and rob our programs--health care and disability compensation--to pay for tax cuts for the wealthy."

21 year old, Jay Briseno from Manassas Park, Va., was in Baghdad on a sweltering afternoon in June 2003 when out of nowhere a bullet pierced the back of his neck. The army rushed Briseno to one hospital after another, saving him from multiple heart attacks and strokes until finally he stabilized enough to be shipped back stateside. Briseno is a high level quadriplegic tethered to a respirator forgotten by the war that rages on without him, chewing up other young men and women,

leaving them equally destroyed. His care was left to his parents and sisters initially as all struggled to adjust. His father, Joe quit his job to be with his son. "From the beginning all we got from the VA was lip service. They questioned every piece of equipment we asked for. They told us Jay should be in an institution. They told us to give up on him. We were desperate when these people from the Army called and said, Do you have what you need? Is there any way we can help?" Thousand's like the Briseno family will be forced to navigate the difficult and often frustrating course of learning about the benefits and services of disabled veterans. With ongoing cuts to the VA and benefits for veterans, the fight to maintain services for those returning from the Iraq and Afghanistan war is has and will be an uphill battle for our nation's veterans.

A few weeks after the Iraq invasion and just 3 days before President Bush spent the Memorial Day weekend thanking the nation's veterans for their service; he proposed slashing Veteran's health care by $1 billion in 2004. An administration memo proposed a 3.4 percent cut in the Veterans Administration budget for 2005, from $29.7 billion to $28.7 billion, this follows other cutbacks since the Decider became president. It is not that there is a lack of funding for the military, in fact this year we will spend $16.9 billion more on military increasing funding to $399.1 billion dollars. America spends more on military spending than the combined annual spending of the next 18 nations combined. In Bush's 2007 budget funding for Veterans increased from current year $24.5 billion, to $27.7 billion, however, the medical services budget faces a 3 percent cut in 2008 and would hover below $27 billion for the next four years, even as increasing numbers of veterans from the Iraq war claim their benefits and the costs of providing care to elderly World War II and Korean War veterans continue to rise. "Those cuts would prove traumatic to the already troubled VA medical system, and would force staff cuts, delay investment in new medical equipment and deny care to hundreds of thousands of veterans."

For decades, the Veterans Administration has struggled to keep up with providing health care to the 7.5 million veterans enrolled. At any one time, more than 3,000 vets await their first visit to the doctor. Those whose injuries from battle qualify them for disability compensation wait six months to two years to receive it. Veterans of the Iraq and Afghanistan wars have waited 54 days on average to get their first veteran disability compensation checks. With VA's costs increasing by 10% to 15% a year and newly disabled veterans draining resources the system is under a serious strain. According to David Uchic, spokesman for Paralyzed Veterans of America says the military cannot keep up with the number of soldiers returning wounded and needing benefits."It doesn't just end with them going to Walter Reed [Army Medical Center in Washington] and being treated. This is a lifelong situation for them for the next 60 to 80 years. So is the system going to be ready to serve them for all those years? That is the question." A recently released Harvard University study "shows the hidden financial costs of the Iraq war will be felt for decades." Researchers estimate that medical costs for U.S. veterans of the wars in Iraq and Afghanistan will be at least three hundred fifty billion dollars over the next forty years and that the total medical costs could reach $660 billion dollars. The only way we as a nation can honor, support, and protect our wounded soldiers from unnecessary struggle is by demanding Congress to stop funding the war and support Veterans' health and benefits. We must stop the insane escalation especially now that the Bullseye is on Iran. If we attack Iran, I fear there will be no stopping the next global war.

> "The Party seeks power entirely for its own sake. We are not interested in the good of others; we are interested solely in power. Not wealth or luxury or long life or happiness; only power, pure power....Power is not a means; it is an end. One does not establish a dictatorship in order to safeguard a revolution; one makes the revolution in order to establish the dictatorship.... If you want a picture of the future, imagine a boot stamping on a human face - forever."
> O'Brien to Winston
> George Orwell 1984

-David Dees

Forgotten Heroes: How many are truly injured?
February 16, 2007
Zen Garcia

The question to ask is this: "How many soldiers have been permanently injured from these wars on terror?" The Pentagon separates combat related and non-combat related injury and death so as to hide the truth from the American people. Private military contractors are not included in the official tally of combat related deaths which as of February 10th is 3,377. The official tally however, does not include "non-combat" related injuries, or injuries not the result of enemy fire. The 'official' count of injured in Iraq according to the Pentagon had been 47,000 soldiers in January of 2007. That figure was revised to 32,000 just this month as the Pentagon decided not to include troops who suffered what it considers minor injuries or mental illness in the official tally. The Pentagon is now being accused of under counting the number of troops injured in Iraq and Afghanistan. Some claim the real numbers could be twice what they counted or more.

Bullets, RPG's, and mortar rounds discriminate less about casualty and being killed than our government's definition of being wounded in action. The Pentagon will only recognize a soldier's sacrifice for our country under the strictest mandate and interpretations of what it means to acquire a combat related injury. Take the case of Joel Gomez for instance, Gomez, was riding in the back of a Bradley fighting vehicle hunting insurgents on a dirt road when the ground gave way and they ended up rolling down the mountain. They landed upside-down in the Tigris River. Both of his buddies were killed and Gomez became a quadriplegic unable to move. Though he was in a military situation, doing a mission that was combat related the Pentagon defined him as 'non-combat injured 'and his buddies as 'non-combat related' deceased.

Another example: Chris Schneider, a young Kansas father, part of a Reserve unit providing security for a supply convoy traveling 100 miles through hostile territory, was injured when another convoy of heavy equipment transporters slammed into his truck throwing him 50 feet through the air until he landed on the road. The second transport in that convoy locked up brakes, sliding 50 feet until it came to rest on his pelvis wedging his lower leg into the axle. Schneider now uses an artificial leg and walks with a limp. According to 60 minutes which did an interview with him, he too is not counted on the Pentagon's casualty count.

Though it doesn't make sense to the soldiers that have returned from Iraq, 62 year old civilian Gene Bolles has a good idea. Dr. Bolles has spent two years at the hospital in Landstuhl, Germany, where he specializes in brain and spinal injuries. As a neurosurgeon with 32 years of practice, he admits he has never seen trauma to this degree. He says, "What you see on TV and what you see in reality, is like night and day.

The embedding of the journalists made the war out to be like a football game. The true effects of war are not reported at all. In fact, the Bush administration has forbidden journalists from taking pictures of wounded or dead soldiers or even the hundreds of caskets that have been flown in from war. Many have said that the administration does not want what happened during Vietnam to happen today, that being loss of popular support for the war. Especially in wake of no weapons of mass destruction, no connection to Al-Qaeda, no imminent threat, and the UN stance of the war against Iraq being illegal."

In 2004 60 Minutes asked the Department of Defense for an interview on non-combatant injury totals. The DOD declined but sent a letter alleging "More than 15,000 troops with so-called 'non-battle' injuries and diseases have been evacuated from Iraq." Dr. Bolles countered with claim, "I've seen figures that are now upwards of 30,000. I know that at least 20,000 have been air-evacuated into the Landstuhl system." The current numbers as of February of 2005 according to the Department of Veterans Affairs - 85,000 out of the 360,000 discharged veterans from Operation Iraqi Freedom (OIF) and Operation Enduring Freedom (OEF), nearly one in four have already visited the VA for physical injuries or mental health counseling. 'This number far exceeds the 12,000 wounded reported by the Department of Defense.' America better get ready for a whole population of soldiers that will need lifelong support and long term care to manage quality of life. I ask you for their sake, the sake of the families of these soldiers who fight and fought for our country because they believe and believed in America and the freedoms we once represented to the world.

Call your Representatives and your Senators and tell them to support Veteran's benefits before appropriating any further funds for the wars especially now at a time when so many return with pressing need for that support. We must set-up the support network which will provide them that support without they and their families ever having to struggle fighting the system to get what they justly deserve. Our nation owes them a debt of gratitude and must absolutely and without delay own up to the responsibility of taking care of their needs. It's not their fault they were sent off to fight what they thought was a just war. Now that they have become injured during the process of engagement, our nation must and without question, honor their service by providing all they need for reintegration back into American society. "A people united can never be defeated, a people silenced, can never be heard."

-David Dees

Giuliani vs. the Firefighters: September Criminal or 9/11 Hero?
April 5, 2007
Zen Garcia

Rudy Giuliani's rise to prominent national and world attention was elevated by his role as Mayor of New York City during a time of heightened challenge that culminated in the fateful events of September 11th, 2001. The leadership qualities he exhibited that day won him broad and wide acclaim from the 9/11 commission, "On September 11, 2001, the City of New York showed what it was made of. The heroism of the firemen and the police officers who risked and in previously unimaginable numbers gave their lives in the quest for saving the lives of others, and your leadership on that day and in the days following gave the rest of the nation, and indeed the world, an unvarnished view of the indomitable spirit and the humanity, of this great city, and for that I salute you." Having been established as a hero, Giuliani has been emphasizing his 9/11 status ever since and today is enjoying promising numbers in Presidential polls which opine him as the 'nominee' to beat in '08. He has refined himself as 'America's Mayor,' suggesting that if he can handle the events of that day, then surely as President he could handle anything that might come his way. Many Americans hold Giuliani in high regard, considering him a great leader, a political hero; the type of person who can take charge in a moment's notice and manage when things seem at their worse. This definition has been so ingrained into American society that even the Christian right seems to be willing to support him and his liberal stances on gun control, abortion, and gay civil unions. Giuliani was awarded the title Knight Commander of the Most Excellent Order of the British Empire by Queen Elizabeth II on October of 2001. He was also named one of People Magazine's "25 Most Intriguing People of the Year 2001", Time Magazine's "Person of the Year 2001", and A&E's "Biography of the Year in 2001."

Giuliani's cult hero status went untarnished and unchallenged until he decided to decline an invitation to the International Association for Firefighters Forum, open to all Presidential candidates for Q & A. Mainstream news then picked up on the story and exposed the contention between the former Mayor and the real heroes, the New York Firefighters who lost so many of their friends and compatriots in the attacks of that day. All was not well in Oz and finally someone had alluded to the mask shadowing the truth - a great rift exists between Giuliani and the one group America assumes to be his staunchest allies.

When Giuliani declined their invitation, a letter was e-mailed to all 280,000 members of IAFF-- representing 85% of the nation's firefighters -- indicating that most of the association had not wanted to invite him anyways and then listed why. "The IAFF recognizes that Mayor Giuliani generally enjoys a favorable reputation as a result of his actions immediately after the tragedy of 9/11. Many people consider Rudy Giuliani "America's Mayor," and many of our members who don't yet know the real story, may also have a positive view of him. This letter is intended to make all of our members aware of the egregious acts Mayor Giuliani committed against our members, our fallen on 9/11, and our New York City union officers following that horrific day. Rest assured, our exclusion of Mayor Giuliani is not about any particular contractual or policy issue or disagreement. His actions post 9/11 rise to such an offensive and personal attack on our brother and sisterhood - and directly on our union - that the IAFF does not feel Rudy Giuliani deserves an audience of IAFF leaders and members at our own Presidential Forum. The disrespect that he exhibited to our 343 fallen FDNY brothers, their families and our New York City IAFF leadership in the wake of that tragic day has not been forgiven or forgotten."

What did Giuliani do that so outraged the firefighter's and their families, that they would still hold such a grudge against him 5 years later? One cannot understand the source of this contention unless one has done some real and difficult research into the events of that day. "In November 2001, our members were continuing the painful, but necessary, task of searching Ground Zero for the remains of our fallen brothers and the thousands of innocent citizens that were killed, because precious few of those who died in the terrorist attacks had been recovered at that point. Prior to November 2001, 101 bodies or remains of fire fighters had been recovered. And those on the horrible pile at Ground Zero believed they had just found a spot in the rubble where they would find countless more that could be given proper burial. Nevertheless, Giuliani, with the full support of his Fire Commissioner Thomas Von Essen, decided on November 2, 2001, to sharply reduce the number of those who could search for remains at any one time. There had been as many as 300 fire fighters at a time involved in search and recovery, but Giuliani cut that number to no more than 25 who could be there at once.

In conjunction with the cut in fire fighters allowed to search, Giuliani also made a conscious decision to institute a "scoop-and-dump" operation to expedite the clean-up of Ground Zero in lieu of the more time-consuming, but respectful, process of removing debris piece by piece in hope of uncovering more remains. Mayor Giuliani's actions meant that fire fighters and citizens who perished would either remain buried at Ground Zero forever, with no closure for families, or be removed like garbage and deposited at the Fresh Kills Landfill. .when hundreds of family members of the fallen joined with our affiliate leadership and members to protest Giuliani's decision, he ordered senior officers of the New York Police Department to arrest 15 of our FDNY brothers, including a number of local elected IAFF leaders."

Here is where the mainstream falls short in their reporting: Why would Giuliani all of a sudden forcefully remove Firefighter's from 'the pile' and in such a way that resulted in a brawl between the NYPD and the NYFD? What the mainstream press will never dig into or question is: why did Giuliani place more importance on cleaning up "the pile" than in taking a slow-retrieval approach to accessing the bodies of firefighters, police, and emergency workers still trapped in the wreckage of those buildings? Though 2 months later, chances were that no one was still alive, many still clung to the hope, that loved ones would be dug out of the devastation of those destroyed buildings. Families wanted a chance for closure, bodies of their loved ones returned so that they could honor them with a proper memorial and burial. The friends families of the fallen wanted to take their time in dismantling 'the pile', so that the dead would be respected and given opportunity to be reached and yet Giuliani thought it better to begin a rushed quick dismantling of 'ground zero,' completely disregarding his most important constituency when it comes to reinforcing him as the 9/11 hero he has now determined to take his Presidential stance on.

The firefighters believe that the city went to a 'scoop and dump' policy because they were in a rush to retrieve gold. "The fact is that the Mayor's switch to a scoop-and-dump coincided with the final removal of tens of millions of dollars of gold, silver and other assets of the Bank of Nova Scotia that were buried beneath what were once the towers. Once the money was out, Giuliani sided with the developers that opposed a lengthy recovery effort, and ordered the scoop-and-dump operation so they could proceed with redevelopment." With his training as District Attorney for New York, Giuliani knows from his prosecutor days that the first rule of a criminal investigation is in cordoning off a crime scene and preventing the tampering or removal of any piece of evidence within that area. Usually officers are put in place to prevent the eradication, removal of, or disruption of anything within that scene. Surely the events of September 11, 2001, constitute the most egregious, barbaric, terroristic, and criminal act ever perpetuated on American soil.

Bill Manning, editor of Fire Engineering, a 125-year-old-monthly firefighting trade magazine with ties to the New York City Fire

Department, wrote in an editor's opinion piece in the January 2002 issue called "$elling Out the Investigation", "Fire Engineering has good reason to believe that the 'official investigation' blessed by FEMA and run by the American Society of Civil Engineers is a half-baked farce that may already have been commandeered by political forces whose primary interests, to put it mildly, lie far afield of full disclosure." He also called for an immediate stop to the removal of steel from the site of ground zero saying the steel from the site should be preserved as a crime scene so that investigators can examine what caused the collapse and pass that knowledge on to future generations of engineers. The editorial continues, "A growing number of fire protection engineers have theorized that 'the structural damage from the planes and the explosive ignition of jet fuel in themselves were not enough to bring down the towers," the editorial stated.

And yet rather than preserve that scene or allow the emergency workers to search for their fallen comrades, Giuliani instead brought in the NYPD to seal off the area and minimize any search and rescue work. He was in a rush to start dismantling ?the pile' siding with developers and agreed to a plan to sell off the scrap metal to foreign nations for even cheaper than what they could have sold it for here in the States. Why go through the trouble of shipping scrap metal out of country if you do not have something to hide? "New York authorities' decision to ship the twin towers' scrap to recyclers has raised the anger of victims' families and some engineers who believe the massive girders should be further examined to help determine how the towers collapsed."

When police officers began forcefully removing firefighters from the scene, a brawl ensued between the two departments. "Five police officers were injured during the protest, Police Commissioner Bernard Kerik said, adding that there could be more arrests. The 10 firefighters arraigned Saturday _ including three union officials _ were charged with criminal trespassing. Some were also charged with obstructing governmental administration and harassment. Earlier charges of inciting to riot, a felony, were dropped." Giuliani then claimed that the process of cleanup needed to be expedited for the sake of the firefighters, and when that didn't work, the excuse was the need for the quick construction of a memorial of some sort or another building, and yet neither of those things happened. Ground Zero still remains an empty space for the shortened lives of restless ghosts, and broken families.

``We were given very, very strong advice that this site was a disaster waiting to happen," Giuliani said. ``Our concern has to be for the lives of the people who are working there now." Firefighters claimed that more than 200 of their comrades were still buried in that rubble and that they wanted to recover the remains of their fallen with dignity. "Giuliani modified his policy after the protest because public opinion was so strongly with our members. Ultimately, he was forced to put the fire fighters back on the pile. Our protests were later proven justified as more bodies were ultimately recovered and those families given a chance for closure and a decent burial. 2007 and bones are still discovered all the time at site.

"Giuliani argued that the change was for our own safety, but his argument was empty and without substance. Fire fighters had been on that pile since minutes after the twin towers fell - why all of a sudden, after nearly two months working on the pile, was Giuliani concerned about fire fighter safety? "Firefighters' have an honor code much like that of the military in that they leave no one behind. "Recovering even a piece of a turnout coat or helmet gave our FDNY brothers and sisters and the families of the fallen some small semblance of peace, something to honor. But hundreds remained entombed in Ground Zero when Giuliani gave up on them. The fundamental lack of respect that Giuliani showed our FDNY members is unforgivable - and that's why he was not invited. Our disdain for him is not about issues or a disputed contract, it is about a visceral, personal affront to the fallen, to our union and, indeed, to every one of us who has ever risked our lives by going into a burning building to save lives and property."

The mainstream press also assumes gold as the reason for the 'scoop and dump' policy, yet my investigation hints to another cover-up. Giuliani and the city of New York spent $1000 on individual GPS navigation systems, to tag wreckage and insure its traceable delivery to barges which would expedite the disappearance of meaningful evidence. Never in the history of fire has any steel structured building lost structural integrity due to flames and yet on 9/11/2001 we had 3 buildings "collapse' in perfect synchronous style, only WTC 1 and 2 were hit by airliners, WTC 7 also 'collapsed' and still no 'official' answers as to why? One must ask why Giuliani and the city would spend all that money just to tag and trace every piece of wreckage leaving the site and then go through what seems unnecessary trouble to ship it abroad. The drivers who drove this wreckage out were told not to detour from their destination, and not to stop, not even to use the bathroom. "Ninety-nine percent of the drivers were extremely driven to do their jobs. But there were big concerns, because the loads consisted of highly sensitive material. One driver, for example, took an extended lunch break of an hour and a half. There was nothing criminal about that, but he was dismissed."

The Family Steering Committee of Families of 9/11 Victims and the American public drafted a list of questions for the 9/11 Commission when they found out that Giuliani was to testify before a panel on May 19th, 2004. The very first question on their list of real questions to be asked was this:

"1. A few short weeks after 9/11, tons of metal from the collapsed twin towers was sold to scrap yards in New Jersey. Thereafter, the steel was re-sold to other recyclers in the United States and overseas. Anecdotal evidence suggests that the "scrap" has ended up in India, Japan, South Korea, China and Malaysia. It is the FSC's position that the thousands of pounds of debris was crime-scene evidence. It should have been examined, cataloged, and stored in a secure location. Why were the steel beams sold and shipped overseas and not retained as evidence? Was the material examined before it was sent overseas? If examined, then by whom? Were any diagnostic studies/tests performed? If not, then why? Whose responsibility was this? Former FBI Acting Director Thomas Pickard said that the FBI wanted to take over Ground Zero and make it a crime scene as was done at the Pentagon. If that had occurred all materials from the scene would have been protected until an investigation was complete. Pickard also stated that you, Mayor Giuliani, would not allow the FBI access to the pit area. Is this accurate? If so, then what was your reason for keeping the nation's chief investigatory team the FBI, out of Ground Zero?"

The question was never asked of the former Mayor by his friends on the 9/11 Commission. Answers were never really sought out fully. Audience members accused the Commission of whitewashing the truth and heckled it to ask real questions, some were forcefully removed. It is my opinion that Giuliani's team assessed the risk and decided it best for him to skip out on attending the IAFF's Presidential forum, concluding it best to avoid the IAFF's questions altogether. Why should he give someone a real opportunity to ask him a real question like how FEMA knew to be in New York on September 10th or who at the Office of Emergency Management had warned he and others that the South Tower and World Trade Center 7 were 'about to collapse' when no building ever in the history of fire had ever before collapsed as a result of the loss of structural integrity?

Giuliani stated in an ABC News interview that he was given warning of a collapse well in advance of the actual event. I was "told that the World Trade Center was gonna' collapse," referring to the 9:59 destruction of the South Tower. "I went down to the scene and we set up a headquarters at 75 Barkley Street, which was right there with the Police Commissioner, the Fire Commissioner, the Head of Emergency Management, and we were operating out of there when we were told that the World Trade Center was gonna' to collapse. And it did collapse before we could actually get out of the building, so we were trapped in the building for 10, 15 minutes, and finally found an exit, got out, walked north, and took a lot of people with us."

His account is corroborated by 2 different eye witness accounts from the passages of the Oral Histories of emergency responders. The account of EMT Richard Zarillo goes as follows: As I was walking towards the Fire command post, I found Steve Mosiello. I said, Steve, where's the boss? I have to give him a message. He said, well, what's the message? I said the buildings are going to collapse; we need to evac everybody out. With a very confused look he said who told you that? I said I was just with John at OEM. OEM says the buildings are going to collapse; we need to get out. He escorted me over to Chief Ganci. He said, hey, Pete, we got a message that the buildings are going to collapse. His reply was who the f___ told you that? Then Steve brought me in and with Chief Ganci, Commissioner Feehan, Steve, I believe Chief Turi was initially there, I said, listen, I was just at OEM. The message I was given was that the buildings are going to collapse; we need to get our people out. At that moment, this thunderous, rolling roar came down and that's when the building came down, the first tower came down."

Zarillo's recollection is verified by Fire Marshall Steven Mosiello's account: "At that point I don't know exactly when the Commissioner and Mayor had left. It was pretty soon after they had left that Richie Zarillo, who works with EMS -- I believe he's an OEM liaison -- came running up to me. I was not on the ramp at this time. I was like almost at the sidewalk location. He said Steve, where's the Chief? I have to tell him, you know -- I said tell him what, Richie? These buildings are in imminent danger of collapse. I said how do you know that, you know? So he ran with me. I ran over and grabbed Chief Ganci and said Chief, these buildings are in imminent danger of collapse."

If Giuliani knew the towers were 'to collapse' as he said he did, why not order emergency and rescue workers out of the buildings and save some of the 403 first responders that were killed on that day? The real question is: who in the OEM told Guiliani and Zarillo that the towers were pending collapse? If someone had prior knowledge of the towers destruction, perhaps that person can explain how they knew those towers were coming down. Something is amiss. How can we as a nation allow our government to wage a 'war on terror' that they promised us 'will not end in our lifetimes' based on events that were never fully investigated? Did Guiliani decline the IAFF's invitation because he was afraid that somebody would expose his legacy and that would warrant further investigation? If he can keep up the mirage of himself as the great leader then he may just successfully hi-jack the reigns of Executive power. After all, many still consider him a 'hero of that day' and regard him with the highest esteem.

What I want to know is: Will America really allow Giuliani to succeed the Decider as Fuhrer? Do you really want to give this man, above the law executive privileges when he still holds the answers to so many questions which still need to be answered? Too many questions still need to be asked of the events of 9/11. The real questions have yet to be explored, and the real investigation still awaits to be done. I leave you with the words of a protester escorted away from the 9/11 Commission proceedings when he demanded the right to ask Giuliani some real questions before he extracted from the proceedings, "Remember this, your government funded and trained al Qaeda. Your government funded and trained al Qaeda. I'll say it one more time. Your government funded and trained al Qaeda."

-David Dees

The Trumpet Sounds: People of the World Unite
July 26, 2007
Zen Garcia

I think it's important to say as an American who only wishes peace and prosperity for everyone everywhere that the general population of hard-working, family loving, God fearing people only want the same for the people of the world as they want for themselves --life liberty and the pursuit of happiness. The people here truly have a good heart and want what is best for everyone everywhere. We wanted our government to use the dream of America to expand the bounty of abundance not gluttony but abundance to every man woman and child everywhere.

The people here believe in the Constitution and the Bill of Rights; and want those same courtesies and bled for rights to be extended to all nations everywhere. We wanted a republican form of government to represent the desires and wishes of all the people gathered within our boundaries. America in her purest ideal wishes justice, rule of law, equal citizenship, freedom to all who respect and uphold the same rights for all people everywhere. We respect and believe in human rights, health care, education, opportunity, bounty for all.

People of the world know that we as a collective people do not support the current tyranny masquerading as government. We do not support this idiot president dancing on a string. We do not support the gluttonous oil baron occupying the vice presidency. We do not support the lying incompetent poster girl traveling around as the Secretary of State. We do not support any of the fascists Council on foreign relations bidding Neo-con hawks trying to start World War III. Nor do we support this impeachment is off the table, do nothing, bend over and take it in the rear Democratic Congress now shafting the people courting corporate interests.

We want accountability as much as the people of the world. We would love nothing more than to bring all of the crooked evil slimy serpents masquerading as politicians in every slot of government to court and expose all of their dirty little secret lives. The traitors are installed inside the halls of Congress, the barbarian hordes are inside the Gates, and all of the people are steady sleeping hoping things will stay as they are for at least one more day. It's not going to hold up this dream of America and the way things had once been.

The government is too evil and the people too complacent; the two together make a fine recipe for a little order out of chaos the New World order freaks so adamantly desire. I still hope and pray every day that the powers that be do not succeed in pulling off another false flag terrorist event and reign in their plans for martial law. I pray to the Lord every day to forgive the sins of the nation and the sins of its people and especially the sins of its government. I pray that the people of the world understand that the people of America do not hate the people targeted by our government for war.

Some do, no doubt, but those that do their homework and understand what's really going on -- that governments all over the world stage their own fear mongering events against their people to initiate and create support for a particular agenda that is usually contrary to the will and desire of the people everywhere abroad, do not support the policies of the government and how could they. How could any of us when we realize that our governments are torturing people, practicing genocide, funding terrorism, assassinating political leaders, harassing and disappearing people whenever they want wherever they want simply because they can.

It's always problem reaction solution-- that's the MO of the corporate elitist Bilderberg new world order zero population control freaks trying to bring in world government. People of the world we need your help to help ourselves. Spread the word that we are fighting as hard as we can on the inside to wake up our own citizenry. Please do the same there.

Want to know why the United Nations fails everything when it comes to human rights and equal citizenship for all people. It's because the United Nations is the strong arm of the global corporate elitist agenda? The people that make the decisions at the top are only trying to bring in a global police State to oppress the peoples of the world and steal as much of the world's remaining natural resources as they possibly can to further enrich their all ready wealthy systems of control. Do your homework people, the lives of all of us depend on it.

"Today, America would be outraged if U.N. troops entered Los Angeles to restore order [referring to the 1991 LA Riot]. Tomorrow they will be grateful! This is especially true if they were told that there were an outside threat from beyond, whether real or *promulgated*, that threatened our very existence. It is then that all peoples of the world will plead to deliver them from this evil. The one thing every man fears is the unknown. When presented with this *scenario*, individual rights will be willingly relinquished for the guarantee of their well-being granted to them by the World Government." Dr. Henry Kissinger, Bilderberger Conference, Evians, France, 1991

-David Dees

Can Cindy Sheehan save America?
August 15, 2007
Zen Garcia

We hold these truths to be self-evident, that all men are created equal, that they are endowed by their Creator with certain unalienable Rights, that among these are Life, Liberty and the pursuit of Happiness. - That to secure these rights, Governments are instituted among Men, deriving their just powers from the consent of the governed, - That whenever any Form of Government becomes destructive of these ends, it is the Right of the People to alter or to abolish it, and to institute new Government, laying its foundation on such principles and organizing its powers in such form, as to them shall seem most likely to affect their Safety and Happiness.

"At least forty-five people were arrested on Capitol Hill Monday in a sit-in calling on Democrats to pursue the impeachment of President Bush and Vice President Dick Cheney. The demonstrators were jailed after refusing to leave the office of House Judiciary Chair John Conyers following a meeting with him. Conyers had floated the idea of impeachment last year. But House Speaker Nancy Pelosi dismissed the talk during the mid-term elections when she declared that impeachment is off the table," said Amy Goodman of Democracy Now, the day that Cindy Sheehan announced that she would challenge Nancy Pelosi for her previously uncontested congressional seat. Cindy was one of the 45 arrested at Conyers office in Washington D.C.

Sheehan was the catalyst for an impromptu vigil to Crawford, Texas, where she sat in a ditch for weeks trying to force a meeting with the decider. She had one question, "What was the noble cause that her son had died for in Iraq?" Obviously, the decider couldn't dream up a noble cause because he refused to meet with Sheehan. It wasn't 2 months earlier that Sheehan stepped away from being the 'face' of the anti-war to refocus her life and priority. Now back to challenge democratic support of Bush administration policies, Sheehan said, "The country is ripe for a change. It's going to start right here and right now." Sheehan said she would run as an independent on a platform of universal health care, making college affordable and improving ethics in the legislative and executive branches, and accountability.

I thought what better way for the American people to express their absolute disgusts with Pelosi and Democratic support of Bush administration policies than to remove by popular vote the highest-ranking Democrat for backing a policy of continuous unobstructed and unabated war advertised to not end during our lifetimes. Not only have the Democrats extended the war without deadlines or limitations, they've given the Decider the green light to spy on American citizens. They have signed off on the illegal and immoral extension of torture, rendition, and dismantling of habeas corpus.

I called Pelosi just to say, remember Rick Santorum, remember George Allen, both of these high ranking Republican Senators thought they too were above reproach, and continued to push for policies unfavorable to popular opinion --the lost their office and the same can happen to you and all of the other bought and paid for political hacks. We the people put you into power to do one simple thing -- end the illegal and immoral war against Iraq and its people.

Prudence, indeed, will dictate that Governments long established should not be changed for light and transient causes; and accordingly all experience hath shewn that mankind are more disposed to suffer, while evils are sufferable than to right themselves by abolishing the forms to which they are accustomed. But when a long train of abuses and usurpations, pursuing invariably the same Object evinces a design to reduce them under absolute Despotism, it is their right, it is their duty, to throw off such Government, and to provide new Guards for their future security

We have been seven years into a war that should never have happened and should not be allowed to conclude one minute longer. The Democrats could have forced the president to utilize the money that was in the pipeline, to the begin the withdrawal. They have and had the power to suspend funding the war and yet did not. They did make a big show about how hard they tried before they rolled over to assume the position. I see no better way to send a message than by voting out of office the one politician that could and did take impeachment off the table. Never before in the history of this great nation has a criminal administration ever been so deserving of impeachment as the one occupying the White House right now. Not only is she refusing to investigate this corrupt tyranny parading around as government, she is refusing to allow others like John Conyers to do it themselves.

Cindy Sheehan and has done more for America in one summer and one year then most of the lifelong politicians occupying public office in Washington, DC. We need representatives with backbone to stand up for the Constitution. We need a presence in Congress that cannot be compromised or paid off, someone like Paul Wellstone the former senator from Minnesota before his untimely 'accidental' death. All of our basic rights and freedoms are being obliterated to nonexistence. The America we grew up with is no longer the America that our children will inherit.

He has refused his Assent to Laws, the most wholesome and necessary for the public good.

What America has to realize is that there is no left right Democratic Republican Liberal conservative two-party system working together for the benefit of our great nation. There is a one party system of bought and paid for politicians bowing to the whims of the fascist corporate elite that supports the destructive open border free trade policies pushed by the Executive. The two parties are just different sides of the same coin and unless America recognizes that, citizens will not know who the enemy is and why bringing in a new party does nothing to change policy.

We need to vote out all of the lifelong politicians except maybe a few. I say vote them all out and make them re-earn our trust. It is up to the people to make the difference. I support Cindy Sheehan's efforts to oust Nancy Pelosi from her congressional seat and I support average Americans taking it upon themselves to run for office and be of public service. We must support representatives that are reflections of ourselves, who truly know the lives that we struggle with every day. As long as the game is set up so that only rich people can run for office, the people at large will never truly be represented unless by luck or by fate someone with honor, integrity should win office.

He has dissolved Representative Houses repeatedly, for opposing with manly firmness his invasions on the rights of the people.

We need an educated, invigorated citizenry to shake up the game of American politics by becoming actively involved in and knowledgeable about all the issues. We need to force them to have real debate and answer real questions. For this we need a citizen media, armed with camera and attitude for willing confrontation. We need youth involvement and empowerment. This is your world being screwed up. This is your country being destroyed. We must correct the image of America by reasserting those values and freedoms that we not so long ago represented to and were symbolic of. We cannot be a nation of torture, extraordinary rendition, indefinite detention, and coerced testimony.

He has obstructed the Administration of Justice by refusing his Assent to Laws for establishing Judiciary Powers.

The only way that this nation can once again become great, is for the people to take it upon themselves to restore order to the constitutional checks and balances between the branches of government. We must restore integrity back to the executive and judicial branches of government. We must be able to believe what our leaders say. Our leaders' words must stand for something. There must be accountability. And the only way that will happen is for this sleepy citizenry to wake up from slumber and rise to the call of duty. You are needed now more than ever. Patriots arise to serve your country because if you arise not now, there may be no America to defend.

We hold these truths to be self-evident, that all men are created equal, that they are endowed by their Creator with certain unalienable Rights, that among these are Life, Liberty and the pursuit of Happiness. ? That to secure these rights, Governments are instituted among Men, deriving their just powers from the consent of the governed, That whenever any Form of Government becomes destructive of these ends, it is the Right of the People to alter or to abolish it, and to institute new Government, laying its foundation on such principles and organizing its powers in such form, as to them shall seem most likely to affect their Safety and Happiness.

"One of the least understood strategies of the world revolution now moving rapidly toward its goal is the use of mind control as a major means of obtaining the consent of the people who will be subjects of the New World Order."
From The National Educator, K.M. Heaton

-David Dees

What's It Going to Take America?
August 22, 2007
Zen Garcia

What's it going to take America, for you to see that our country is imploding, that our system of governance is corrupt beyond repair, and that our elected officials are all bought and paid for? Will it take the drowning of another city, the collapse of another major bridge system, the explosion of another refinery, or will it be another major 9/11 false flag terrorist event initiated by some rogue elements within our own government to spur support for the war of terror on terror. There is no longer time for complacency, or idle threats; now is the time for action. It's now or never.

Ask yourself, if there really is a war on terror why not implement the 9/11 commission recommendations for securing our nation? Why are the borders still wide open and ports unsecured? Why does the Bush administration continue to push free trade policies with Communist China when one of their generals threaten to nuke 200 of our cities two summers ago? On August 10, 2007 they threatened to dump their surplus of dollars to purposely collapse the American economy. If China wants to nuke the US or collapse our economy, why does Bush continue to grant them favorable trade policies when American workers and American jobs and American consumers all suffer from not only the loss of production but also from the low quality standard of products being imported from China? Seems every night something newly imported from China has been found to be contaminated with very strange toxicity such as the toothpaste recall that found anti-freeze and brake fluid within the ingredients. We cannot forget the thousands of beloved American pets that suffered miserable deaths due melamine tainted pet food. Many varieties of imported farm bred Chinese fish were banned from import because of toxicity levels. Now we have a whole host of children's products being recalled due to lead toxicity. The question I have, is this ignorance or purposefully orchestrated attempts to poison the American people?

Now the Bush administration wants to allow the Chinese government to process our poultry and ship it back to American shores. When will the lunacy end? When are the American people going to act and declare enough is enough? We know the FDA has no concern for safeguarding the American food supply and neither has the budget nor the staff to conduct a proper monitoring of consumer goods flooding into the American market.

We should be supporting American manufacturers, American farmers, here in our own country where we can regulate the standards and quality of of products being sold to our communities but no, instead we support our own destruction by purchasing the flood of slave goods from foreign countries where labor and quality standards are mostly nonexistent to Wal-Mart shelves where people think they get good deals because of cheap prices.

Now that American roads and critical infrastructure are being privatized and sold off to foreign investment consortiums, Americans are finally displaying outrage at the thought of foreign companies owning parts of our country. Just as in the Dubai ports deal, states and counties across the nation are revolting against public official's attempts to sell off highways and other toll roads to companies who have no vested interest in maintaining the integrity of that infrastructure for the American people. We have seen time and time again when it comes to privatization and for-profit ventures how it is the public that suffers the consequences of those policies.

If Americans are so outraged at foreign nations being allowed to purchase American infrastructure, just think what would happen if they knew that our entire monetary system was usurped by a Federal Reserve Board made up of foreign banking interests. What would happen if Americans learned that the all powerful Fed was neither a government nor a federal agency and that the money taxed for wages and earnings went not to pay for the infrastructure, education, health care, or government systems but to pay down the interest on the debt from the Federal Reserve printing the money and loaning it to our government at interest.

The Constitution calls for Congress to maintain the monetary system and yet on December 23, 1913 the international bankers were allowed to hijack the nation's monetary system. They have stolen the wealth of America ever since and used it to enslave the world. These same bankers are close to bankrupting the American economy now in support of a Pan American Union and a new Amero currency. The only way we will be able to stop them is if we abolished the Federal Reserve System and the IRS. One of the reasons I support Ron Paul for President is because of his efforts to abolish this criminal system. For more information about this watch Aaron Russo's new film America: Freedom to Fascism.

Our country is near bankrupt. Bush has borrowed more money than all other presidents combined. Our nation has already committed to spending over $1 trillion to support the illegal and immoral wars that we know we were duped into supporting. We are already spending 25% of our total GDP just paying down the interest on this debt. How much more have these wars cost us when you consider the degradation of American infrastructure, the cost of not covering our children and citizenry with adequate and preventative healthcare? What is the cost of not funding the proper education of our children? What will be the cost of allowing our borders to remain wide open, our air and water ports insecure? What will be the cost of America's loss of reputation and standing in the world? Bush has done irrevocable damage to this country and who knows what the costs of that will be in the future.

Will America rise to speak out when the terrorists start to blow up things here in our own country? Will it then not be too late? Do you know that we are being left open to attack so that America can be scared into giving up more rights and more beloved freedoms? Do you know that your government and governments throughout history have funded and allowed attacks to go forward just so that they can legitimize increasing budgets to fight terrorism and institute police state measures which only increased the monitoring tracing and tracking of the entire public abroad.

August 3rd, 2007 on Democracy Now, Amy Goodman interviewed Jim Ridgeway in his written a piece for Mother Jones about how the FBI not only knew beforehand that there was a terrorist plot against the Oklahoma City federal building but that they allowed the attack to go forward, and even covered up links to their involvement within the plot. Shortly after the Oklahoma City bombing the Justice Department under Waco Reno asked for a 13.7 percent increase in the FY 1997 budget to reduce violent crime, drugs, terrorism, and illegal immigration.

"To most people the 1995 Oklahoma City bombing is a closed case. Timothy McVeigh and his accomplice Terry Nichols were the two prime suspects accused. McVeigh was executed in 2001, and Nichols is serving a life sentence. But a Salt Lake City lawyer searching for the truth behind his brother's death has uncovered a wealth of new information that could implicate the FBI. The documents he dug up through countless Freedom of Information Act requests suggest the FBI knew about the plot to bomb the Alfred P. Murrah Federal Building in advance but did little to prevent it."

If you study the incidents of the 1993 world trade Center bombing you find the same modus operandi - "In February 26, 1993, a car bomb at the World Trade Center in New York City, New York, exploded, killing six people, injuring thousands and causing extensive damage. The FBI quickly arrested four radical Muslims, who were convicted in 1994. More members of the radical group were tried beginning January 16, 1995, for a wide-ranging plot of terrorist attacks. One reason the FBI was able to act so quickly is that an FBI informant was the one who built the bomb. The U.S. government paid the informant, Emad Salem, $1 million for his testimony. Salem tape-recorded conversations with the bombing suspects. Unbeknown to the FBI, Salem also recorded his conversations with them. The FBI benefited greatly from the World Trade Center bombing. In particular, the bombing resulted in the proposal of the 1995 Counterterrorism Bill greatly expanding federal authorities' budgets and powers."

Those with the eyes, ears, and mind for discernment are trying to give those interested in truth the key to deciphering the propaganda parading as reality. America and her military are being destroyed on purpose. You cannot have a strong America in a Pan American union where all nations bow to world government. You cannot have an Amero currency unless the dollar and the total economic structure is devastated. You cannot have forced debt internment upon a people that can easily care for, protect, and secure its citizens; thus the destruction of the middle class by the kingly dictatorial monarchy running our government. The executive branch has been compromised for decades and with it the peoples power to manage a truly representative form of government. With the power of executive veto and privilege the enemies of our country have always controlled how legislation is drawn up and it is only when the people have had enough and take to the streets that we slow down their agenda for a restored monarchy and total dictatorial rule.

"The UN is but a long-range, international banking apparatus clearly set up for financial and economic profit by a small group of powerful One-World revolutionaries, hungry for profit and power."

"The depression was the calculated 'shearing' of the public by the World Money powers, triggered by the planned sudden shortage of supply of call money in the New York money market....The One World Government leaders and their ever close bankers have now acquired full control of the money and credit machinery of the U.S. via the creation of the privately owned Federal Reserve Bank." - **Curtis Dall, FDR's son-in-law, in his book My Exploited Father-in-Law**

-David Dees

Open Martial Law Coming to America
August 27, 2007
by Zen Garcia

On September 19th, Senator Patrick Leahy (D-Vermont) declared his reservations about the 2007's Defense Authorization Act which contained a "widely opposed provision to allow the President more control over the National Guard [adopting] changes to the Insurrection Act, which will make it easier for this or any future President to use the military to restore domestic order without the consent of the nation's governors. We certainly do not need to make it easier for Presidents to declare martial law.

Invoking the Insurrection Act and using the military for law enforcement activities goes against some of the central tenets of our democracy. One can easily envision governors and mayors in charge of an emergency having to constantly look over their shoulders while someone who has never visited their communities gives the orders." We saw the consequences of a Fed takeover of a disaster in wake of the aftermath of Katrina in which Blackwater was hired to patrol American streets with American tax payer money. Illegal evictions and gun confiscations took place while citizens were allowed to die in the streets waiting for the government to help in some way. Citizens cannot rely on government to help out in dire circumstances. Everyone certainly knows that the decider does not care to help in a time of tragedy. He doesn't even care to prepare for disasters. Hell, he won't even secure the borders. Should we trust him when we are the most at risk in a time of vulnerability to send aid when he would not even end his vacation to address the situation in New Orleans and even went to California for a photo op where he was shown playing a guitar while hundreds died in the streets from a lack of basic necessities.

On September 29th, Leahy entered into the Congressional Record that he had grave reservations about certain provisions of the fiscal Year 2007 Defense Authorization Bill Conference Report."Language in the bill, he said, "subverts solid, longstanding posse comitatus statutes that limit the military's involvement in law enforcement, thereby making it easier for the President to declare martial law." This had been "slipped in as a rider with little study while other congressional committees with jurisdiction over these matters had no chance to comment, let alone hold hearings on, these proposals."

Anyone that studies how the Executive has evolved martial law in America will find a long string of Executive orders leading back to Oliver North, Rex 84, and many administrations that have asserted the Executive, the 'privilege' of suspending Constitutional checks, balances, rights, and freedoms. Those that utilize the executive to subvert the people's have since the founding of this country has been trying to restore the dictatorial power of a kingly monarchy which the global elite enjoyed the benefits of for centuries. They have always enabled the 'divine right of kings' as the preferred form of governance because of the ease with which oppression of the masses could take place. They want to be able to subject the masses to their own wishes and agendas, thus the push for world government.

Let me now tell you how close we came to 'martial law being established in America during the events of September 11th, 2001. I present to you these little known facts. On September 11th, at least four other planes were supposed to be flown into targets in America. Speculation has been given to Flight 93 which supposedly crashed in Pennsylvania, but since has been found ordered shot down by a Canadian General on Bush's orders while all other 'hijacked' planes were allowed to reach their target because of the Norad standown. Two grounded Delta flights were found with 'box cutters' placed in the bathroom stalls by what had to be workers of the actual airlines ground crew. "A knowledgeable source said two small knives were found on a Delta flight that was supposed to depart Boston, and a box cutter was found on an Atlanta-to-Brussels Delta flight. These planes didn't take off since all flights were grounded after the hijackings. The tools were found when the planes were searched." We know there were more targets. What were those targets?

The FBI had also investigated another United Airlines flight, scheduled to leave Kennedy International Airport for San Francisco, on September 11, because four Middle Eastern-looking men refused to return to their seats once this particular flight was grounded. They left the plane in a hurry as soon doors were opened insuring escape, and nothing more has since been reported about the flight or the men. "Government sources would not describe in detail the nature of the weapons found on the Delta flights last week, but one official disclosed that another weapon was discovered on at least on other aircraft, owned by a fourth airline. The government official refused to name that carrier." If we consider the possibility of 3 more planes reaching their targets and only one of those targets being the US Congress or Capitol building, our system of government as we know it, would have been effectively and significantly crippled so much so, that government could not go on the way it once had.

During the Zaccarias Moussaoi trial America was informed by one of the supposed hypothetical masterminds behind the attacks of September 11th, 2001, that Flight 93 had originally been intended to hit Congress. "In the final minutes of Flight 93, passengers attempted to retake the plane at which point the hijackers crashed it into the western Pennsylvania field. The plane had been headed for the U.S. Capitol; according to Sept. 11 mastermind Khalid Shaikh Mohammed." Take this testimony into account with the fact that already in place, was a plan signed by Congress to give dictatorial power to the executive branches of government, meaning the president in times of uncertainty where martial law must be declared; would assume dictatorial powers.

This scenario would have definitely occurred if the Capitol had been hit and the majority of members killed. Why do I believe martial law was the intended consequence for the United States post September 11th? Two sources released a little discussed story of how one hundred of the Republican leaders from all branches of government had already been moved to a bunker and were prepared to take over duties as the official government from that bunker. No Democrat or Independent was invited or even notified including the Minority leadership. It was not until the story was reported by the press that the Democrats learned of the existence of this shadow government.

Should the attacks on America been fully successful, America would already be under open "martial law" rather than the covert one we now find ourselves in. Can you imagine if an airliner dove into the Congress and devastated that seat of government? The Neo-Con Hawks would then have had no problem continuing America unimpeded down the road of imperialistic empire expansion as called for by the Project for a New American Century call for global domination. They are pushing us into a 3rd global crusader war which will bring the whole world to its knees. Once this atrocity is accomplished they believe the world will cry 'peace, peace' at which time they will unveil their false Christ to bring that peace to the global community through world government. Order out of chaos, the Illuminati have been planning it for years.

Albert Pike, founder of the Ku Klux Klan, received a vision, which he described in a letter that he wrote to Mazzini, dated August 15, 1871. This letter graphically outlined plans for three world wars that were seen as necessary to bring about a New World Order through a one world government. "The Third World War must be fomented by taking advantage of the differences caused by the "agentur" of the "Illuminati" between the political Zionists and the leaders of Islamic World. The war must be conducted in such a way that Islam (the Moslem Arabic World) and political Zionism (the State of Israel) mutually destroy each other. Meanwhile the other nations, once more divided on this issue will be constrained to fight to the point of complete physical, moral, spiritual and economical exhaustion. We shall unleash the Nihilists and the atheists, and we shall provoke a formidable social cataclysm which in all its horror will show clearly to the nations the effect of absolute atheism, origin of savagery and of the most bloody turmoil. Then everywhere, the citizens, obliged to defend themselves against the world minority of revolutionaries, will exterminate those destroyers of civilization, and the multitude, disillusioned with Christianity, whose deistic spirits will from that moment be without compass or direction, anxious for an ideal, but without knowing where to render its adoration, will receive the true light through the universal manifestation of the pure doctrine of Lucifer, brought finally out in the public view. This manifestation will result from the general reactionary movement which will follow the destruction of Christianity and atheism, both conquered and exterminated at the same time." The 3rd global crusader war started with the deceit of 9/11.

Do you see now why we cannot, must not be complacent anymore? We must demand accountability through impeachment or America as we knew it, will be lost forever.

Men like your father, the hidden masters of finance capitalism, govern those who govern, produce, and think through invisible financial tentacles, the operations of which will be elucidated later by my colleagues. Dominance in all aspects of society is surreptitiously accomplished while the great majority of the ruled, and even most of the visible leaders, believe themselves to be fairly autonomous, if harried, members of a pluralistic society. – The Occult Technology of Power

-David Dees

Domestic Spying and the Banning of Dissent?
October 12, 2007
Zen Garcia

In 1933, the Nazi SS established Dachua as the first concentration camp to house thousands of German political prisoners, whose ideas and belief systems were considered a threat to the then authoritarian regime. At first, mainly Jewish authors and artists whose words and works were considered subversive were subjected to arrest, economic restrictions, and various forms of harsh discrimination. The earliest targets for Nazi persecution in Germany were political opponents-- primarily Communists, Socialists, Social Democrats, and trade union leaders identified by a large secretive domestic spying program which monitored the activities of the populace for the Nazi SS. The program was later expanded to include people with disabilities, those with homosexual leanings, and anyone else that opposed totalitarian rule.

In September 2002, $64 million dollars in research contracts were awarded to a secretive technology research-and-development office located near the headquarters of the NSA. The office was tasked with developing a program called Novel Intelligence from Massive Data. "NIMD funds research to ... help analysts deal with information-overload, detect early indicators of strategic surprise, and avoid analytic errors," reads a "Call for 2005 Challenge Workshop Proposals" released by the Advanced Research and Development Activity (ARDA). The program is used to sort through the massive collections of data mining databases already developed and convert them into usable intelligence for federal agencies.

Governments have always used combating enemies - like communism or terrorism - while using fear to justify the loss of liberty. The Nazi's also targeted citizens in the guise of protecting the common good from "terrorists and terroristic elements." The domestic spying program of today is a rehash of the Nixon era attempt to assert executive privilege over the lives of ordinary citizens while using fear to convince the public that such a program is for our own security.

As in the late 1930's, the government is clandestinely developing databases on those groups and individuals who know about and dissent against corrupt governmental policies and the emergence of a fascist police control state. While Americans believe government is utilizing the warrant-less spying program to target "Al-Qaeda", citizens' advocacy and government watchdog groups have challenged the government's authority to spy on its citizens in court by citing countless FOIA requests which verify under judicial review, that the government has and still does utilize millions of dollars of taxpayers own money to pursue countless intelligence hours to task the infiltration surveillance and monitoring of political ecological antiwar peace loving groups and citizens unions. Just who does the government think the enemy is?

On November 14, 2001, Angel Shamaya released an article entitled "Public Servants" Going After "Constitutional Terrorists"? which specifies, according to a Phoenix Federal Bureau of Investigation flyer released at the Arizona "Freedom in the 21st Century" gathering, just who the government considers domestic terrorists. Called the Joint Terrorism Task Force, the flyer details an effort by the FBI to "work jointly with local law enforcement."

The flyer specifically identifies and targets subversive elements the government considers 'domestic terrorists and domestic terrorism.' The brochure begins "If you encounter any of the following, call the Joint Terrorism Task Force," and then proceeds in setting forth guidelines which law enforcement officers should look for when identifying 'domestic terrorists or terrorism' including such things as: "Right winged extremists" or "Super Patriots or defenders of the US Constitution against the federal government and the United Nations." Groups of individuals involved in Paramilitary training. "Hate groups" such as black separatists' and even those with a "Christian Identity." "Common Law Proponents" who make "numerous references to the U.S. Constitution", "anyone who asks the law enforcement officer to cite his authority for making a stop", anyone who says driving is a "right," and not a "privilege", and or someone who attempts to "police the police."

These are not the only groups identified in the flyer but certainly the most shocking since American citizens who know their Constitutional rights are clearly labeled domestic terrorists by the flyer. Put into context with the Patriot Act, a domestic terrorist is essentially an enemy combatant and enemy combatants have no right to even know why they've been detained and can according to the Military Commissions Act, can be indefinitely held, tortured, and even convicted using that coerced testimony.

Just what is the government doing with the databases it is developing on its own citizens? If you don't know already, it's all about developing and implementing a complete tracking and tracing system for monitor of not just terrorists but all people entrenched within the system. The global elite want a complete system of tracking for not only the global population but every commodity sold on the global market.

On October 4th, 2007, Mark Nestman released an article called, "Soon You'll Have To Ask Permission Before You Fly." In that article, Nestman discusses the implementation of two Transportation Safety Association passenger approval programs for travel abroad and within the United States. Both systems come online Feb. 19, 2008 after the election. Soon passengers will need the approval of the federal government to leave the country and/or to travel within.

"What this amounts to is essentially a reprise of the infamous 'internal passport' system in effect in the former Soviet Union. In 1933, Soviet dictator Josef Stalin introduced 'internal passports' that prohibited Soviet citizens from leaving their place of residence without permission. Over time, the internal passport became the prime instrument of Soviet oppression over its citizens. It's bad enough needing to ask Uncle Sam for permission to leave the United States, and to reenter it. But an internal passport is a blueprint for totalitarianism." Under the TSA's APIS - Advance Passenger Information System, one will need permission from the U.S. government to travel on any commercial airliner, ship, or vehicle that enters, goes through, or exits the United States even if it is just for a layover enroute to another foreign destination. One will not receive permission to board and travel until cleared by TSA. Whether a U.S. citizen or not, everyone must obtain permission to enter - or leave - the United States."

Another program called "Secure Flight" will require all commercial airlines to submit passenger validation through both the Secure Flight and APIS programs before approval for travel. The Department of Homeland Security who heads up validation of both programs will be the determining factor when it comes to approval for travel whether domestically or abroad. If you are denied permission to travel as two leading U.S. peace activists were Wednesday, October 3rd, you have no recourse but to beg to be allowed to travel.

Retired Army Colonel and Diplomat Ann Wright was traveling with Medea Benjamin, co-founder of women's peace group CODEPINK, were headed to Toronto to appear at an antiwar event when they were denied entry into Canada because of their names appearing on an FBI Terrorist watch list. "In my case, the border guard pulled up a file showing that I had been arrested at the US Mission to the UN where, on International Women's Day, a group of us had tried to deliver a peace petition signed by 152,000 women around the world," says Benjamin. "For this, the Canadians labeled me a criminal and refused to allow me in the country."

"The FBI's placing of peace activists on an international criminal database is blatant political intimidation of US citizens opposed to Bush administration policies," says Colonel Wright, who was also Deputy US Ambassador in four countries. "The Canadian government should certainly not accept this FBI database as the criteria for entering the country." Both Wright and Benjamin plan to request their files from the FBI through the Freedom of Information Act and demand that arrests for peaceful, non-violent actions be expunged from international records. "It's outrageous that Canada is turning away peacemakers protesting a war that does not have the support of either US or Canadian citizens," says Benjamin.

Do you think we are far off from American dissidents being 'extraordinarily renditioned' and disappeared? Still think the program is about targeting 'terrorists'? Do you now realize what's going on and if you do realize, do you now know that you too are in danger of being pinpointed by the domestic spying program?

Where does it go from here? Who knows but I expect things will get a lot worse before they get better. God help us all.

> **The so-called Left-Right political spectrum is our creation. In fact, it accurately reflects our careful, artificial polarization of the population on phoney issues that prevents the issue of our power from arising in their minds. The Left supports civil liberties and opposes economic or entrepreneural liberty. The Right supports economic liberty and opposes civil liberty. Of course neither can exist fully (which is our goal) without the other. We control the Right-Left conflict such that both forms of liberty are suppressed to the degree we require Our own liberty rests not on legal or moral "rights," but on our control of the government bureaucracy and courts which apply the complex, subjective regulations we dupe the public into supporting for our benefit . – The Occult Technology of Power**

-David Dees

Why Did John Kerry Concede So Quickly in 2004?
October 25, 2007
Zen Garcia

Recently Paul Craig Roberts said in an article entitled, "America is No More," Naïve Americans who think they live in a free society should watch the video filmed by students at a John Kerry speech September 17, Constitution Day, at the University of Florida in Gainesville." The video depicts John Kerry picking a 21 year old journalism student, Andrew Meyer for question.

Bearing a copy of Greg Palast's book, Armed Madhouse, Meyer asked if Kerry was aware that Palast's investigations determined that He and not the decider had actually won the election? He also asked why Kerry conceded the election so quickly when there were so many obvious examples of voter fraud and disenfranchisement. Meyer also confronted Kerry on his refusal to consider Bush's impeachment especially now that the whole world knows that Bush has been planning for possible preemptive nuclear strikes against Iran?

For exercising his First Amendment right to free speech and assembly, Meyer was quickly surrounded by police, seized, tasered, and then arrested on bogus charges. All this because of asking an uncomfortable question to the Senator or was it something more? Why not answer the question? It's not like the rest of us haven't wondered the same thing. I have had that question in mind since the night of November 2nd, 2004 when Kerry came out and conceded to his cousin and fellow skull and bones secret society member George W Bush. It was not an hour earlier that vice presidential candidate John Edwards gave speech to the media and the people that they meaning he and Kerry would not concede the election until every vote was actually counted.

It was all so obvious to the world and to anybody that closely followed the elections, that fraud was rampant and everywhere prevailing. The 2004 election results could have been rightfully contested for months following the results of that night and yet John Kerry conceded without even all of the Ohio provisional votes being fully counted. The provisional ballots could have easily won him the election. Paul Craig Roberts contended, "The question we should all ask is why a United States Senator just stood there while Gestapo goons violated the constitutional rights of a student participating in a public event, brutalized him in full view of everyone, and then took him off to jail on phony charges?

Kerry's meekness not only in the face of electoral fraud, not only in the face of Bush's wars that are crimes under the Nuremberg standard, but also in the face of police goons trampling the constitutional rights of American citizens makes it completely clear that he was not fit to be president, and he is not fit to be a US senator. Usually when police violate constitutional rights and commit acts of police brutality they do it when they believe no one is watching, not in front of a large audience. Clearly, the police have become more audacious in their abuse of rights and citizens. What explains the new fearlessness of police to violate rights and brutalize citizens without cause? The answer is that police, most of whom have authoritarian personalities, have seen that constitutional rights are no longer protected. President Bush does not protect our constitutional rights. Neither does Vice President Cheney, nor the Attorney General, nor the US Congress. Just as Kerry allowed Meyer's rights to be tasered out of him, Congress has enabled Bush to strip people, including American citizens, of constitutional protection and incarcerate them without presenting evidence."

Like Andrew Meyer, I too wondered why Kerry would rush to concede when the hope of the world was concentrated behind him. The whole world was ripe and begging for change, praying that the American people would vote in that change. The 2004 election had an atmosphere of prevailing possibility and unimaginable hope. The need for changing direction pervaded the dreams and prayers of people all over the world who wished for nothing more than peace on earth, goodwill to all people, and the end of Bush tyranny.

All of that energy dissipated when Kerry said, "Earlier today, I spoke to President Bush, and I offered him and Laura our congratulations on their victory. We had a good conversation, and we talked about the danger of division in our country and the need, the desperate need for unity, for finding the common ground, coming together. Today, I hope that we can begin the healing. In America it is vital that every vote count, and that every vote be counted.

But the outcome should be decided by voters, not a protracted legal process. I would not give up this fight if there was a chance we would prevail. But it is now clear that even when all the provisional ballots are counted - which they will be - there won't be enough outstanding votes for us to be able to win Ohio, and therefore we cannot win this election." Why not wait until at least morning and give it some time to settle out? Wanting to know, I did some research online and somehow came across a C-Span interview in which Alex Jones claimed that not only were both Bush and Kerry cousins from the same family, but both had connections to a Yale secret society death cult called Skull and Bones. It was then that I watched all of Alex's documentaries.

By the time I had perused all of that work, I would never again be the same person. It was then that I wrote an article called, "Overwhelming Evidence Suggests Government Complicity in 9/11." "I did not learn the truth behind the events of September 11 until the run up to the 2004 election debacle when Kerry conceded to Bush, and the anti-war movement really had no candidate to support or endorse even though they, like the rest of America, jumped on the "Anything but Bush" bandwagon. Little did I know that both Kerry and Bush were members of a Yale secret society called Skull n Bones, and are cousins by blood relation; then, when I learned about Bush's close connection to the Saudi royal family and in particular the Bin Laden family I really started to look into the events of 9/11. The image of the Twin Towers on fire, smoldering, and then exploding into huge piles of twisted steel, concrete having been blasted into fine powder, are sure signs of explosions.

The fire fighters themselves reported explosion after explosion happening on all levels of the World Trade Center and finally culminating in the demolition of World Trade Center 7 as reported by Larry Silverstein himself in a PBS documentary special saying a decision was made "to pull the building." I, too, like many Americans when initially grasping the overwhelming evidence which clearly demonstrates that a rogue element within our government including the White House and its staff were and are at least partly responsible for allowing the terrorist attacks of 9/11 to be successful, wanted to deny it.

Because of 9/11, they were able to invade Afghanistan and Iraq, and also pass Patriot Acts 1, 2, and now 2.5 which severely erodes the Constitutional liberties of every American citizen. We are now guilty until proven innocent. The establishment of this new homeland security amounts to nothing less than Orwell's "Thought Police" for intelligence gathering. Our right to privacy has been thrown asunder, and the voices of dissent punished as example to others who stand up for our rights. Our government is now openly fascist, directed for the interests of the global international bankers and oil companies like Halliburton. We are invading countries with the sole purpose of stealing their natural resources as proven by passing time. We are utilizing loans from the World Bank to bankrupt nations and place them at our mercy.

However, many parts of the world are not happy with the way things are and have taken it into their own hands to force changes upon the puppet governments that our country has established worldwide. The globalists fear that their plan for a one world government controlled by them through the United Nations Security Council is starting to falter. Already, the French and the Danes have voted down the European Union Constitution fearing a loss of national sovereignty.

America, too, is starting to protest and warn Americans about the planned pan-American union which would merge Canada, the United States, and Mexico. America must support its own national sovereignty in order for us to stay the proud vision of our forefathers as they deliberated upon the foundations of a republic that would keep all its citizens free and protected from the tyrannical elements of a government out of control.

We must, again, empower states and communities at the local level so that communities take care of themselves and look after the economic prosperity of their own neighborhoods and in that way, ensure the security and growth of communities all across America. There are many waking up that now understand the predicament that we find ourselves in. We must, as patriots, warn each other and wake each other up as much as possible. It is necessary for this time that we each share what we know, for in sharing what we know we can turn this country around," seems a little prophetic for June 4, 2005.

Many Americans do not know who Alex Jones is or what his contributions to this country have been. From a personal standpoint I can say that I owe this man a great deal. Alex too was recently harassed and arrested by New York Police Department officers while filming his documentary about the sixth anniversary of September 11th. Jones was protesting the official version of 9/11 with a crowd of 400 other truth activists. According to Infowars sources Jones was singled out by police, verbally accosted, and forced to present identification which he was not carrying at the time. NYPD officers arrested Jones for "unspecified charges" much like Myer and removed from the crowd and taken to the nearest police precinct where he was later released following a large protest outside the jail by other 9/11 truthers who chanted "let him go". Truly Toto were not in Kansas anymore.

We must stop the collective discrimination of individuals and groups that hold opposing opinion to the agenda of this corrupt and criminal administration. If they will already openly harass and lockup intellectuals, it is just a short distance to kidnapping and disappearing individuals as they already do in other parts of the world. Alex knows that he's a target, but he also knows what kind of world the globalists want our children to live in. He knows that if he does not put himself on the line and nobody else does, there is nothing standing in the way of a one world order United Nations global police State awaiting the people of the world. And that's no world anyone other than the rich elite would want to live in.

Many of us have now awakened to the realization that terrorist elements exist within our own government. That in itself is a scary thought to comprehend. It is frightening to ponder and yet that is the reality that truth leaves with you. Those that awaken to truth can never ever return to the bubble safe sense of reality that we had once lived in. For me I would rather know the truth no matter what that truth is. As in the early years of Nazi Germany, intellectuals are targeted because of the knowledge they possess.

Knowledge is power.

Knowledge is what informs people about the truths of reality. Without the watchman without the informers, there is no informed citizenry. Intellectuals are the last bastion of a free press which truly informs the people. The reason that anti-government policy groups are targeted by government is because they/we represent a threat. That threat is the organizing structure and capacity to unify people no matter what the cause, and affect change by applying political pressure in mass numbers. It has always been divide and rule.

The more the powers that be, can separate people along differentiating lines, the easier to control the minority fragments. It is only when people work together to settle those differences and come together in a cohesive force that things truly get done. It is obvious that we cannot rely on our representative leaders to hold themselves accountable for actions and behaviors while in public office. Most would sell us out for minuscule amounts of cash or favor. Because of this we are at the point now in our nation's history where everybody must make a choice to act.

There may be no tomorrow for us to demand accountability if we do not now confront the criminals attempting to bring in world government. The world will rise up against the United States unless we change things from within and end the wars of terror destroying our nation, foreign-policy, international alliances, reputation, and credibility. Please pray for our nation and world; we need all the help we can get. More than anything act, act, and act to save our nation. Patriots you are needed now more than ever.

> "I think Skull and Bones has had slightly more success than the mafia in the sense that the leaders of the five families are all doing 100 years in jail, and the leaders of the Skull and Bones families are doing four and eight years in the White House,"
> — Ron Rosenbaum, columnist for the New York Observer, quoted in CBS News' report on Skull & Bones, June 13, 2004

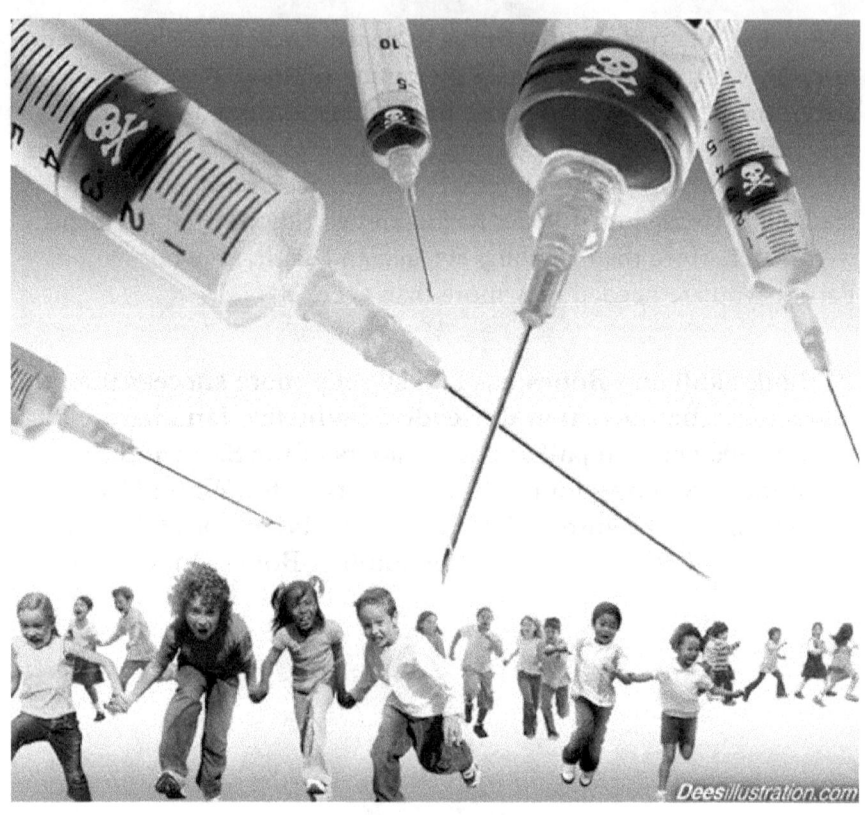

-David Dees

Jenny McCarthy vs. the CDC
November 10, 2007
Zen Garcia

It was four o'clock sun still bright and warm to feel; my personal attendant Charlotte was inside watching Oprah Winfrey as she normally does about that time. She called me excitedly and said, "Zen you have got to come see this." I was reluctant to leave the warm embrace of afternoon light but situated myself on the front porch so that I could hear the show while continuing my work outside. Oprah had as guests Jenny McCarthy and Holly Peete and they were discussing the topic of having a child with autism.

There is a quiet epidemic in America, over 40 million mothers and families are dealing with the epidemic of having a child or several children with autistic characteristics or symptoms of Asperger spectrum disorders. I having been an anti-vaccine, anti-thimerosol advocate for many years became keenly interested in the show when Jenny McCarthy openly blamed the vaccinations that her child received at 18 months for stealing the life out of her child. She said that once her child received those vaccines that it was like lights out for her young son, Evan.

I became really excited because finally the truth was coming out and on a show that reaches 50 million families across the world. I have been an anti-vaccine advocate ever since I wrote an article on the subject for a disability magazine years ago. In that article entitled, "Vaccine Preservative Thimerosal and the Destruction of an Entire Generation of Americans Kids," I detailed the fact that Eli Lilly had known since initial testing of thimerosol in the 1930s that there was and is no safe application for the ingredient. However, a cover-up of the results ensued and Eli Lily successfully lobbied the FDA to be allowed to market thimerosol to American consumers. Over decades now they have successfully expanded the product base in which thimerosal is used. However it should never have come to market to begin with.

"Internal documents reveal that Eli Lilly, which first developed thimerosal, knew from the start that its product could cause damage -- and even death -- in both animals and humans. In 1930, the company tested thimerosal by administering it to twenty-two patients with terminal meningitis, all of whom died within weeks of being injected -- a fact Lilly didn't bother to report in its study declaring thimerosal safe. In 1935, researchers at another vaccine manufacturer, Pittman-Moore, warned Lilly that its claims about thimerosal's safety "did not check with ours." Half the dogs Pittman injected with thimerosal-based vaccines became sick, leading researchers there to declare the preservative "unsatisfactory as a serum intended for use on dogs."

Another undeniable fact that thimerosol is the cause of autism is the fact that an entire population of people exist right here in the America that do not have exposure to or problems with autism. While vaccine makers scramble to protect themselves from such allegations, Dan Olmstead did a series of articles for United Press International, entitled "The Age of Autism" in which he investigated the Amish population of Ohio and Pennsylvania, searching for medical staff or families comfortable with talking about the autistic experience.

He wanted to know if the Amish community would reflect the national average of 1-in-166 when it came to neurological Autism Spectrum Disorders. The Amish do not vaccinate their children so if the thimerosol in the vaccines is and was not responsible for the autism epidemic among the general public, and some genetic factor is involved in the passing of autism from one generation to the other; there would and should be a similar ratio of autism and Asperger's spectrum disorders reflected in the Amish population.

Olmstead wrote on June 14, 2005, - Readers of this column have reacted strongly to our series of reports on autism among the Amish. So far, we have found only a handful of cases of autism and have quoted some experts who think it is nearly non-existent in this group." The Amish of Lancaster County, Pennsylvania, refuse to immunize their infants. Olmsted calculated that there should be 130 autistics among the Amish. He found four - one exposed to high levels of mercury from a power plant and the three other children that had received their vaccines.

Why on Earth the medical establishment would mandate injecting through vaccinations the second most toxic substance of the planet besides those that are radioactive into a child that has not even developed immunity just absolutely makes no sense. The fact that parents simply trust the medical doctors without researching the ingredients in the vaccines is also equally ridiculous. Anyone that studies the ingredients contained within any vaccine but especially those tainted with thimerosol, would not if they had any lick of common sense knowingly inject these poisons into one's own body but especially not their child's.

I know myself beyond a shadow of a doubt that thimerosal also leads to dementia and Alzheimer's in the elderly and that all of us have heavy metal toxicity to some degree. The great thing about mercury toxicity is that it is easily treatable through a noninvasive form of chelation therapy in which a cream or mud is applied to the skin, allowed to dry, and in that way draws out heavy metals through the pores resulting in the detoxification of the body. Chelation has been used to treat lead poisoning since the 1960s.

I have been trying to share this information with people for years but was confronted with resistance every step of the way. I finally resorted to just putting the information out there and hoping the American public would catch on. That is why I was overjoyed to see this information coming to light on the Oprah Winfrey show especially since millions watch her every day. I was excited for the mothers and the families and individuals that would be helped by this information.

I knew however that the fight was just beginning for Jenny McCarthy. Now that she and her organization had challenged the powers that be, they would be targeted, vilified, and harassed much like I was when I came out on this issue. It wasn't but a couple days after Jenny openly blamed vaccinations for her son's autism that the CDC released another bogus study backing up two previous bogus studies which claim that there is no link between autism and vaccinations.

What Jenny, Holly, and Oprah might not know is that the CDC is knowingly lying and being purposefully deceptive on this issue. Melissa Ross released an article called, "CDC Knew of Potential Link between Vaccines, Autism" in which she details how "the Centers for Disease Control published a study repudiating any possible link between thimerosal and developmental problems like autism in children while at the same time knowingly had data supporting such a link-- but kept it from the public." Documents released through the Freedom of Information Act, detail the transcript of a meeting held in June of 2000 between members of the CDC, the FDA, and representatives from the vaccine industry.

The group discusses the results of a February 2000 study that finds a significant association between exposure to thimerosal-containing vaccines, and developmental issues like autism in children. Some of the comments-- "There are just a host of neurodevelopmental data that would suggest we've got a serious problem." "My gut feeling? It worries me. I don't want my grandson to get a thimerosal-containing vaccine until we know better what's going on." "We are in a bad position from the standpoint of defending any lawsuits." Finally-- "We have asked you to keep this information confidential."

And that's what happened. Three years later, the CDC published a study in the November 2003 issue of "Pediatrics" contradicting the earlier results, and clearing thimerosal of any link to neurological problems in children. Instead of coming clean the CDC with the blessing of vaccine manufacturers decided upon a course of action to protect big pharma by covering up the link between autism and vaccines. The vaccine manufacturers then lobbied Bill Frist to quietly slip in immunity for them into a Homeland Security bill passed several years back.

"Senate Majority Leader Bill Frist, who has received $873,000 in contributions from the pharmaceutical industry, has been working to immunize vaccine makers from liability in 4,200 lawsuits that have been filed by the parents of injured children. On five separate occasions, Frist has tried to seal all of the government's vaccine-related documents -- including the Simpsonwood transcripts -- and shield Eli Lilly, the developer of thimerosal, from subpoenas.

In 2002, the day after Frist quietly slipped a rider known as the "Eli Lilly Protection Act" into a homeland security bill, the company contributed $10,000 to his campaign and bought 5,000 copies of his book on bioterrorism. The measure was repealed by Congress in 2003 -- but earlier this year, Frist slipped another provision into an anti-terrorism bill that would deny compensation to children suffering from vaccine-related brain disorders." said Robert Kennedy Jr. in his article "Deadly Immunity."

This immunity prevents them from being sued by families and individuals that have suffered unimaginable disruption to their lives and the lives of their children. You really cannot put a price on that and yet they were successful in getting it signed into law. This action alone should let you know that there is something to the link between autism and vaccines. If there is no link why the need for immunity and why specifically President Bush would veto a bill that would ban mercury in flu vaccines for children.

The White House stated that President Bush would veto the FY 2008 HHS-Labor-Education Appropriations Bill because of the cost and "objectionable provisions" such as a measure to ban the use of childhood flu vaccines that contain thimerosal. An Autism advocacy group Safe Minds warns: "Under the current administration, mercury has been and will continue to be knowingly injected into the youngest of American citizens.

The controversial mercury-containing preservative thimerosal has been linked by thousands of parents as being the cause of their children's mercury poisoning and autism." The flu vaccine, which continues to be manufactured with mercury, is recommended for all pregnant women, infants and children despite the fact that the Institute of Medicine in 2001 recommended against the policy of exposing these same sensitive groups to thimerosal containing vaccines.

On May 21, 2003, after a three year investigation, "The Mercury in Medicine Report" was released by the House Committee on Government Reform, and stated in part: "Thimerosal used as a preservative in vaccines is likely related to the autism epidemic. This epidemic in all probability may have been prevented or curtailed had the FDA not been asleep at the switch regarding a lack of safety data regarding injected thimerosal and the sharper eyes of infant exposure to this known neurotoxin. The public health agencies' failure to act is indicative of institutional malfeasance for self protection and misplaced protectionism of the pharmaceutical industry."

The Congressional report also said that the CDC, due to its "biases against theories regarding vaccine-induced autism," had chosen to fund researchers "who also worked for vaccine manufacturers to conduct population-based immunologic studies. . ." and stated: "The CDC in general and the National Immunization Program are particularly conflicted in their duty to monitor the safety of vaccines, while also charged with the responsibility of purchasing vaccines for resale as well as promoting increased immunization rates."

I was thrilled to see Jenny McCarthy pushing the autism/mercury issue on Larry King a day after the Oprah show. I felt hopeful that the mainstream would have to readdress the story. And they did, many news sites invited discussion on their forums, so I began posting articles I had written about this issue for years everywhere I could find a discussion about the topic. I kept checking back on the sites I posted information to see if my articles would lead to any real dialogue about the issue but noticed that about four hours after posting information for others to learn the things that I know, I found my posts totally scrubbed and eradicated from the sites.

This happened to me on both ABC and MSNBC news bulletin boards. Like years before I was censored. I even posted a couple of times to the same bulletin boards to see if they would scrub my work again but this time I took screenshots to see just how long it would take them. They did quick work as my post only lasted four to five hours before they were wiped clean and the information disappeared.

Those that know thimerosol causes autism like myself were attacked as conspiracy theorists and paranoid whack jobs by the mainstream press and whereas our posts are quickly scrubbed, those posts that support the CDC mainstream position quickly accumulated on the boards. I can't believe that people still think that the mainstream press is out there to provide you data to be an informed citizenry. Wake up people. They're all about controlling what is known, keeping the people stupid, and fleecing us for as much money as they can. Big pharma is a big budget advertiser, and we all know that the customer is always a number one. Do your homework people - your lives, but especially your children's lives, depend on it.

> "If vaccines are so effective in preventing disease why have epidemics occurred around the world following mass vaccination programs? In the Philippines for example, 'after ten years of compulsory inoculation against smallpox (25 million shots) over 170,000 got smallpox and 75,000 deaths were recorded between 1911 and 1920'."
> **- Townsend Letter for Doctors, Feb/Mar 1994**
>
> "Early in this century, the Philippines experienced their worst smallpox epidemic ever after 8 million people received 24.5 million vaccine doses; the death rate quadrupled as a result."
> **- Dr. William Howard Hay's address in 1937, printed in the Congressional Record**
>
> "There is no evidence whatsoever of the ability of vaccines to prevent any diseases. To the contrary, there is a great wealth of evidence that they cause serious side effects."
> **- Dr. Viera Scheibner, PhD**

"This report describes six mothers who received live virus vaccines and one who received a Hepatitis B vaccine during pregnancy after having received an MMR booster five months prior to conception. All the children who resulted from these pregnancies have had developmental problems, six out seven (85%) were diagnosed with autism, and the seventh seems to exhibit symptoms often associated with autistic spectrum disorders."
- Dr. F. Edward Yazbak, MD

"My suspicion, which is shared by others in my profession, is that the nearly 10,000 SIDS deaths that occur in the United States each year are related to one or more of the vaccines that are routinely given children. The pertussis vaccine is the most likely villain, but it could also be one or more of the others."
- Dr. Robert Mendelsohn, MD

"Crib death was so infrequent in the pre-vaccination era that it was not even mentioned in the statistics, but it started to climb in the 1950s with the spread of mass vaccination against diseases of childhood."
- Harris L. Coulter, PhD

"These data show that DPT vaccination may be a generally unrecognised major cause of sudden infant and early childhood death, and that the risks of immunisation may outweigh its potential benefits. A need for re-evaluation and possible modification of current vaccination procedures is indicated by this study."
- Dr. William C. Torch, MD, Director of Child Neurology, Department of Paediatrics, University of Nevada School of Medicine

-David Dees

An Appeal to Our Active Duty Soldiers
November 27, 2007
Zen Garcia

Honoring Veterans: Some reflections on our recent Veterans' Day

Would you allow foreign armies to kick in your doors, detain your family members indiscriminately, rape, brutalize, and torture your neighbors, friends, and family members without regard? Would you not, if that happened in America, create, lead, or join some kind of resistance or insurgency to combat the situation?

My father, a Viet Nam vet, like soldiers of today, almost paid the ultimate sacrifice of duty to our country - his life, having been overrun by Viet Cong outside the province of Dau Teng during the height of the 1968 Tet offensive, the soldiers that did survive that assault forever count themselves among the lucky, living on bonus time.

The best man I've ever known, it wasn't 30 minutes before writing this that he called to tell me that he was lying dormant in a hospital bed struggling with a heart to weak to hold a steady rhythm. Veteran's Day, I wanted to honor him and our soldiers, memorializing his contribution and our veterans' contributions to our flag.

Sunday, a church bell sounds from nearby sanctuary where people congregate to praise the greatness of our Lord and Creator, Son having died on the cross to defeat death and bring salvation to the world. I pray for my father's healing and quick recovery as I pray for the protection and quick return of our soldiers spread everywhere across the world fighting to uphold duty and honor in attempt to protect family and loved ones at home from ever having to experience the front-line horrors of war.

This day we remember the fallen, praising our active duty soldiers especially those returning with life long disabilities or entombed in flag draped casket. And though they are flown in under the cover of night with the honor of press coverage being banned by the decider who doesn't want the public to know how many die daily, Bush cannot hide the staggering numbers of returning veterans struggling to manage return to civilian disability.

Bush cannot hide the number of families and loved ones that have endured loss and are everywhere weeping. He can't hide the staggering numbers of veterans, 1 out of every 4 homeless sleeping on the streets. He cannot hide nor deny the staggering amount of soldiers returning home hopeless in their appeal to get help for what they've gone through.

It was just revealed that there is an epidemic of suicide among returning veterans. 17 of which take their lives daily doubling the average rate of suicide in America. "The US military is experiencing a 'suicide epidemic' with veterans killing themselves at the rate of 120 a week; according to an investigation by US television network CBS. At least 6,256 US veterans committed suicide in 2005 -- an average of 17 a day -- the network reported, with veterans overall more than twice as likely to take their own lives as the rest of the general population."

We, the public, must do something to honor all the veterans for their duty to our country, for believing in and holding affirm to those principles which lead our patriarchs to rebel against domineering forces which neither cared for nor catered to the peace, prosperity, or benefit of the people.

"We hold these truths to be self-evident, that all men are created equal, that they are endowed by their Creator with certain unalienable Rights, that among these are Life, Liberty and the pursuit of Happiness. - That to secure these rights, Governments are instituted among Men, deriving their just powers from the consent of the governed, - That whenever any Form of Government becomes destructive of these ends, it is the Right of the People to alter or to abolish it, and to institute new Government, laying its foundation on such principles and organizing its powers in such form, as to them shall seem most likely to affect their Safety and Happiness."

I honor our veterans as I honor my father for his service to this nation in a time of war. He was proud to wear the uniform and did so for 20 years. For him it was a badge of commendation symbolizing duty to a nation that was a bastion of human rights and protecting freedoms for the people of the world. America had once represented what was right, lawful, and just in the world. We were the hope, inspiration, and envy of people everywhere oppressed by tyrannical forces. We were the catalyst for their struggle to throw off enslavement and take up the struggle for freedom, independence as our forefathers had in forming this once great nation.

The soldier is representative of those traits which led once ordinary citizens to find courage enough to rebel against unimaginable odds endure unimaginable struggle in defending, and upholding the dignity of the collective regard. This nation was born on the bodies of fallen comrades, brothers and sisters in arms who refused to allow themselves to be dominated by autocratic rule and controlled by the whims of despotic monarchs like King George.

How strange that history so often cycles in seemingly similar circumstance. It is in the spirit of righteousness that I appeal this day to the sunshine soldier and the pitchfork patriot willing to take up whatever tool necessary to support the defense of this nation against all enemies foreign and domestic. Please soldier question yourself now -- are the leaders guiding a corrupt and criminal foreign-policy worthy of directing the oath of your allegiance? If you and the citizens of this nation were lied to, scared, and threatened into waging war against a sovereign nation which had nothing to do with the insidious attacks of September 11, 2001, wouldn't that negate the noble cause that the decider claims his war is and make us the enemy instead of the liberator.

It was our previous leaders, presidents, and administrations who supported Saddam Hussein and the Taliban, propping them up as puppet rule. It was American taxpayer money that asserted their power, financially backing their regimes, and arming them to wage war on their neighbors and even their own citizens.

We were both lied to by the same people that now sound the drums of war against Iran. The same lies are being rehashed just in a new way. Question yourself soldier -- do they deserve the power to put your life and that of hundreds of thousands of your friends and citizens into danger just because they want to deny Iran their Non-Proliferation Treaty right to create civilian nuclear power? Did they deserve the right to put you and your fellow comrades into danger in attempting the occupation of the nation with the second largest oil reserves in the entire world which neither attacked us nor had anything to do with Al-Qaeda?

The CIA established Al-Qaeda as a boogey man, a ghost to give our military the necessary enemy for wars of conquest and the expansion of Empire. Dear soldiers, we know that you are good citizens who only wanted to service our country and nation by doing those things which preserved our collective peace and freedoms but please question yourself, can you truly look upon the Iraqi people with hate and disdain for rising up against our military occupation of their country especially in light of the atrocities that private military contractors have and are routinely subjecting their populations to?

Would you allow foreign armies to kick in your doors, detain your family members indiscriminately, rape, brutalize, and torture your neighbors, friends, and family members without regard? Would you not, if that happened in America, create, lead, or join some kind of resistance or insurgency to combat the situation?

The citizens of this country do not blame you in the least for what has happened to Iraq. You were lied to as we were lied to as the world was lied to. All we asked now is that you question yourself about whether your leaders deserve your trust and allegiance. We ask you to resist should they ask you to perform an act contrary to your duty as a soldier in protecting the values that America holds so dear.

Ask yourself also if they had your best interests in mind then why use depleted uranium which puts you, your comrades, and Iraqi citizens at risk for terrible health consequences? Why honor a civilian leadership that will not even fund fully and properly the Veterans Administration, on which you and so many of your brothers and sisters are returning home with lifelong debilitating and permanent disabilities depend.

The leadership guiding you and your friends to unnecessary and tragic deaths, themselves elected to refrain from service to our nation in a time of war when they had ample opportunity to do as you do now. However they used their political connections or legislative loop holes to escape from having to fight in the front lines of war. They do not know what it is like to be on the battlefield with brothers dying around you.

They have no idea what it's like to have to sleep in a foxhole with one eye open for spotting enemy. They have no idea what it's like to see your friend and fellow soldier blown to pieces before your eyes. they have no idea what it's like to be forced by circumstance to shoot down a civilian or child. I myself do not know these things and could never truly understand what hell you have had to go through for your nation.

But unlike them, I would never claim the authority or responsibility to lead you in a time of war when I myself do not understand what that exactly entails. That right should be reserved for somebody that knows what it's like to fight by your side and extended only to someone who understands the atrocities on the ground of decisions made in bureaucratic offices in Washington D.C.

The civilian leadership responsible for the atrocity of Iraq and maybe soon Iran, have proven to you, to the country, to the world that they are not fit to lead and to be honored in their decision making capacity. This criminal administration is totally undeserving of being in command of our nation's military and the lives of our most honored guard. They are fit only to be impeached, tried, and hung as the war criminals they are. Our nation cannot stand for torture, rendition, nor for preemptive attacks of conquest and imperialistic expansion at the expense of other peoples and nations of the world.

Remember your oath to support and defend the Constitution of the United States against all enemies, foreign or domestic. Allegiance to a criminal element of governance waging genocidal policy against innocent people is not honor and duty to our nation. Please soldier help us to bring you home and properly fund the health care and long-term assistance that each of you will need in making sense of the war you were just put through.

Help us to stop the flood of money leaving our countries supporting illegal war and threaten to bankrupt our children's' futures. We are on the verge of total economic collapse of the dollar and destruction of the American economy and your leaders say nothing. We are borrowing huge amounts of money our nation may never be able to repay. If we do not hold accountable these criminal politicians now, we may never get chance again and there will never be an America like we once knew for our children to inherit.

On this Veterans Day, I honor you as I honor my father, for duty to me and every member of this great nation. We just simply ask please soldier question your service to leaders who are not deserving of your dedication and moral sacrifice. We ask you to uphold and extend those values, those principles, those freedoms which made our nation great to all people everywhere. May the Lord bless you and your family wherever you may be.

"Prudence, indeed, will dictate that Governments long established should not be changed for light and transient causes; and accordingly all experience hath shewn that mankind are more disposed to suffer, while evils are sufferable than to right themselves by abolishing the forms to which they are accustomed. But when a long train of abuses and usurpations, pursuing invariably the same Object evinces a design to reduce them under absolute Despotism, it is their right, it is their duty, to throw off such Government, and to provide new Guards for their future security."

-David Dees

Media Matters: Fake News and Distorted Truths
December 11, 2007
Zen Garcia

The Federal Emergency Management Association held a press conference on October 23rd, 2007 about efforts made during the California Wildfires in which at least 1,500 homes were destroyed, over 500,000 acres of land burned, 9 people died, 85 others injured, including at least 61 fire fighters. FEMA had given reporters only about 15 minutes prior notice to attend the impending press conference. FEMA then set up a telephone conference line so that reporters could listen in to the conference but not ask direct questions.

Why FEMA would expect journalists to be able to show up at a news conference in which they were only allotted 15 minutes to make and attend doesn't make sense unless their intent was not to have reporters cover the event, but listen in to 'reporters' substituted by FEMA employees readily prepared to stage the press event. In this way, FEMA could control the scope and focus of questioning asked and answers delivered.

FEMA thought they were doing nothing wrong because this is how the government handles newscast, journalists, and the Free Press. Both the questions and the answers are controlled so that the subject matter and delivery of that subject matter are controlled for specific result. I doubt that this 'fake conference' was an accident because government routinely prepares, distributes, and manages fake news events similar to the one put on by FEMA that Tuesday.

When the mainstream news outlets found out that FEMA had staged the event and had their own staff question the leadership about their own performance during the California wildfires, FEMA's fakery and intention to mislead became the highlight story of evening news on every major broadcast across the country. The fact that they held a news briefing with edited script and fake reporters was quickly chastised by every major player in the mainstream press from ABC to Fox News. FEMA external affairs director John Philbin, who was about to start a new role as media chief for the Office of the Director of National Intelligence was denied position because of his central role in the FEMA fake news fiasco.

"I should have cancelled it quickly. I did not have good situational awareness of what was happening," Philbin told CBS in a telephone interview. On October 27th, 2007, FEMA apologized for leading the staged news conference in which FEMA staff posed as journalists while real reporters listened in on a telephone conference line though barred from asking questions.

Vice Admiral Harvey Johnson released a statement on October 26th, 2007 stating:

FEMA's goal is to get information out as soon as possible, and in trying to do so we made an error in judgment. Our intent was to provide useful information and be responsive to the many questions we have received. We are reviewing our press procedures and will make the changes necessary to ensure that all of our communications are straight forward and transparent. At FEMA, our focus is disaster operations and, in this case, it means working closely with the State of California to support their response to the devastating fires.

We're committed to being there for the State and being good partners. In working to do so we did not put enough focus on how we communicate to the public. The real story -- how well the response and recovery elements are working in this disaster -- should not be lost because of how we tried to meet the needs of the media in distributing facts. We can and must do better, and apologize for this error in judgment.

When questioned about the staged event, White House press Secretary Dana Perino said, "It is not a practice that we would employ here at the White House or that we -- we certainly don't condone it. We didn't know about it beforehand. FEMA has issued an apology, saying that they had an error judgment when they were attempting to get out a lot of information to reporters, who were asking for answers to a variety of questions in regard to the wildfires in California. It's not something I would have condoned. And they, I'm sure, will not do it again."

When asked who was responsible? Perino said, "Well, FEMA is responsible. And they have accepted that responsibility, and they issued an apology today. They have admitted that they had an error in judgment. I would agree with that. They've issued an apology. And, you know, you'll have to ask them about why they decided to do that." Whereas the role of the White House press secretary had once been to educate the press and public on information concerning government policies, those that assume that role now realize that they are part of the controlled arm of public persuasion and government delivery of propaganda.

They are asked to cover for the administration and to do damage control when it comes to evading the onslaught of investigative questions that actually uphold the integrity and objective of a free press as envisioned by our forefathers. The Free Press is the only institution protected by the Bill of Rights. Our forefathers knew how important that institution was for maintaining balance between the powers of government and the will of the governed. Little did they know that our free press would become an extension of big brother, big government.

How prevalent are fake news and fake news conferences to the government control of public opinion? Remember, we were led into supporting an illegal and immoral war against an innocent sovereign nation, duped largely in part by the media support for the push for war against Iraq. A recent study by Congressional Democrats found that the Bush administration spent $254 million in its first term on public relations contracts to hire public relations personnel to create 'fake news' casts around certain issues of government concern, nearly doubling what the last Clinton administration spent on 'fake news.'

"Under the Bush administration, the federal government has aggressively used a well-established tool of public relations: the prepackaged, ready-to-serve news report that major corporations have long distributed to TV stations to pitch everything from headache remedies to auto insurance. In all, at least 20 federal agencies, including the Defense Department and the Census Bureau, have made and distributed hundreds of television news segments in the past four years, records and interviews show. Many were subsequently broadcast on local stations across the country without any acknowledgement of the government's role in their production.

This winter, Washington has been roiled by revelations that a handful of columnists wrote in support of administration policies without disclosing they had accepted payments from the government. But the administration's efforts to generate positive news coverage have been considerably more pervasive than previously known. At the same time, records and interviews suggest widespread complicity or negligence by television stations, given industry ethics standards that discourage the broadcast of prepackaged news segments from any outside group without revealing the source."

How are fake news casts generated for public consumption? "They often feature 'interviews' with senior administration officials in whom questions are scripted and answers rehearsed. Critics, though, are excluded, as are any hints of mismanagement, waste or controversy. Segments have been broadcast in some of nation's largest television markets, including New York, Los Angeles, Chicago, Dallas and Atlanta.

An examination of government-produced news reports offers a look inside a world where the traditional lines between public relations and journalism have become tangled, where local anchors introduce prepackaged segments with 'suggested' lead-ins written by public relations experts. It is a world where government-produced reports disappear into a maze of satellite transmissions, Web portals, syndicated news programs and network feeds, only to emerge cleansed on the other side as 'independent' journalism."

Though every mainstream news station was quick to condemn FEMA for producing and putting on a fake news press conference, what they won't tell you is that they routinely and daily broadcast government produced 'video news reports' for content in their newscasts. Many times clips are purposely edited to represent true journalism when in fact they are scripted within intent to purposely persuade thoughts or opinions with certain bias, or specifically designed to inform viewers about a topic with purposeful objective on swaying opinion about subject or issue being described.

Now that media has been consolidated staffs are being purged and large media conglomerates are more and more dependent upon government produced video news releases to spare the expense of actually hiring journalists and reporters to gather news.

In three separate opinions, an investigative arm of Congress that studies the federal government expenditures, the Government Accountability Office has held that government-made news segments constitute "improper covert propaganda even if their origin is made clear to newscasters." Often newscasters are not passing on to their viewing audience the fact that these 'video news reports' are fake and created by government public relations campaigns and not through investigative journalism. "

The point, the office said, is whether viewers know the origin of newscast content. Last month, in its most recent finding, the G.A.O. said federal agencies may not produce prepackaged news reports "that conceal or do not clearly identify for the television viewing audience that the agency was the source of those materials."

>A code of ethics developed for the Radio-Television News Directors Association, the main professional society for

broadcast news directors in the United States clearly states, "Clearly disclose the origin of information and label all material provided by outsiders." Many stations prohibit the use of any outside material but especially entire reports done by public relations personnel and not investigative journalists. Welcome to the real world of Orwell's doublespeak, newspeak, repeat, repeat until it becomes real.

"What does today's media system mean for the notion of an informed public cherished by democratic theory? Quite literally, it means that virtually everything the average person sees or hears, outside of her own personal communications, is determined by the interests of private, unaccountable executives and investors whose primary goal is increasing profits and raising the share prices. More insidiously, this small group of elites determines what ordinary people do not see or hear. In-depth coverage of anything, let alone the problems real people face day-to-day, is as scarce as sex, violence and voyeurism are pervasive."
- Bill Moyers, Media Matters

"There is no such thing as an independent press in America, unless it is in the country towns. You know it and I know it. There is not one of you who dares to write your honest opinions, and if you did, you know beforehand that it would never appear in print... "The business of the New York journalist is to destroy truth; to lie outright; to pervert; to vilify, to fawn at the feet of Mammon; to sell his country and his race for his daily bread. We are the tools and vessels for rich men behind the scenes. We are intellectual prostitutes." - John Swinton, editor of the New York Tribune

-David Dees

Strait of Hormuz - Gulf of Tonkin Revisited
Zen Garcia
January 15, 2008

"Iran speedboats 'threatened suicide attack on US' in Strait of Hormuz" the headlines of the Times Online exclaimed about the so-called incident where 5 Iranian speedboats were said to have threatened American warships with hostile intention. The White House in response issued a stern warning to Tehran claiming that such actions amounted to acts of war. The Pentagon claimed that US forces were only moments away from opening fire on the Iranian speedboats before they veered off and quickly sped away. The video released detailing the muffled exchange of dialogue between the so-called suicide bombers and U.S. Navy personnel were cited as Iran's intent to start a war with America. "We urge the Iranians to refrain from such provocative actions that could lead to a dangerous incident in the future," said Gordon Johnson,

spokesman for the White House's National Security Council. The decider himself boasted to reporters in the Rose Garden, hours before he left for the Middle East to attempt bolstering support for American foreign-policy. "We viewed it as a provocative act. It is a dangerous situation, and they should not have done it, pure and simple."
The video released by the Pentagon relays this exchange:

IRANIAN VOICE: I am coming to you.

US NAVAL OFFICER: Inbound small craft, you're approaching a coalition warship operating in international waters. Your identity is not know. Your intentions are unclear. You're sailing into danger and may be subject to defensive measures. Request you establish communications now or alter your course immediately to remain clear. Request you alter course immediately to remain clear.

IRANIAN VOICE: You will explode after a few minutes.

US NAVAL OFFICER: "You will explode after a few minutes."

Pentagon spokesman, Bryan Whitman said that the American vessels were in international waters, making a normal transit through the Gulf. He boasted that Iranians were operating at distances and speeds that showed "reckless, dangerous and potentially hostile intent. At least some were visibly armed." American mainstream media was quick to pick up the story and relay it to the world without verifying the facts or details behind the Pentagon's claim. This was the same thing they did prior to the Iraq invasion when weapons of mass destruction and mushroom clouds on American soil were also touted in the same fear mongering kind of way.

The reason I titled this article "Gulf of Tonkin Revisited" is because this same exact thing was done prior to the Vietnam War. For those that do not know, the incident in the Gulf of Tonkin which instigated the entire Vietnam War was based solely on a pair of supposed attacks allegedly carried out by naval forces of the Democratic Republic of Vietnam targeting 2 Navy destroyers, the USS Maddox and the USS Turner Joy on August 2 and 4, 1964.

These incidents lead to Congressional passage of the Southeast Asia Resolution, granting Lyndon Johnson authorization to assist any southeastern Asian country whose government was considered threatened by "communist aggression". The resolution gave America and Johnson legal justification for quick involvement in Viet Nam. Recently, in two separate declassified intelligence reports released in 2005 and in 2008, the National Security Agency verified that it was our U.S. Navy destroyer the Maddox which fired first upon North Vietnamese patrol boats. The second report verified that no attack even occurred on August 4 and that both incidents were exaggerated or fabricated to justify American involvement in Vietnam.

"American Planes Hit North Vietnam After Second Attack on Our Destroyers; Move Taken to Halt New Aggression", announced a Washington Post headline on Aug. 5, 1964, followed later the same day by the New York Times headline: "President Johnson has ordered retaliatory action against gunboats and 'certain supporting facilities in North Vietnam' after renewed attacks against American destroyers in the Gulf of Tonkin." It wasn't until 30 years later and 50,000 American soldiers lost, and untold Vietnamese killed that the truth even crept out.

Kurt Nimmo released an article called "Hiding the Gulf of Tonkin Lie" in which he said, "It should come as no surprise the NSC "has kept secret a 2001 finding by its own historian that its officers deliberately distorted critical intelligence during the Tonkin Gulf episode that helped precipitate the Vietnam War," according to the New York Times. "Most historians have concluded in recent years there was no second attack [against US destroyers on August 4, 1964], but they have assumed the agency's intercepts were unintentionally misread, not purposely altered.

The research by Robert Hanyok, the agency's historian, was detailed four years ago in an in-house article that remains secret, in part because agency officials feared its release might prompt uncomfortable comparisons with the flawed intelligence used to justify the war in Iraq, according to an intelligence official."

Here we are in 2008, the Bush administration lied to get us into the Iraq war everybody knows that. What some might not know is that the decider's father also pulled off his own hoax to justify invading Iraq after greenlighting Saddam's own invasion of Kuwait. From an article entitled "How PR Sold the War in the Persian Gulf." "The most emotionally moving testimony on October 10 came from a 15-year-old Kuwaiti girl, known only by her first name of Nayirah. According to the Caucus, Nayirah's full name was being kept confidential to prevent Iraqi reprisals against her family in occupied Kuwait.

Sobbing, she described what she had seen with her own eyes in a hospital in Kuwait City. Her written testimony was passed out in a media kit prepared by Citizens for a Free Kuwait. 'I volunteered at the al-Addan hospital,' Nayirah said. 'While I was there, I saw the Iraqi soldiers come into the hospital with guns, and go into the room where . . . babies were in incubators. They took the babies out of the incubators, took the incubators, and left the babies on the cold floor to die.' Three months passed between Nayirah's testimony and the start of the war. During those months, the story of babies torn from their incubators was repeated over and over again. President Bush Sr. told the story.

It was recited as fact in Congressional testimony, on TV and radio talk shows, and at the UN Security Council. 'Of all the accusations made against the dictator,' MacArthur observed, 'none had more impact on American public opinion than the one about Iraqi soldiers removing 312 babies from their incubators and leaving them to die on the cold hospital floors of Kuwait City."

Did you know that the heart wrenching story of abandoned babies dying on a cold unforgiving floor was given by the daughter of the ambassador to Kuwait a personal friend and confidant of George Bush Sr. and that Nayirah was a member of the Kuwaiti royal family. Kuwaiti investigators even released their own findings on the report and called it completely fabricated and that she had not even been in Kuwait during the alleged time of the incident.

It didn't matter, the press played up her story, George Bush Sr. repeated her allegations over and over and Congress justifying action gave him narrow authority for the invasion of Iraq in the first Gulf War. Our own Senators and Representatives knew also that Nayirah was the daughter of the Kuwaiti ambassador and that the story was a complete myth, but went along with it for personal benefit.

This past Thursday Iran released its own version of the video detailing the incident in the Strait of Hormuz which verifies that the Pentagon account may have been doctored to justify military action against Iran. Much like the supposed funneling of Iranian armaments into Iraq to kill American troops, the Bush administration is trying everything they can to persuade the public that Iran is a threat to its neighbors.

Do you know that Iran has not invaded any of its neighbors in over 2000 years and only fought a war with Iraq because of American support of Saddam Hussein, who was then still a puppet of the US and waging war at our behest so America can profit at the expense of Middle Eastern blood. What's different now?

Besides how are we to justify a war with Iran when a couple of speedboats armed with nothing but machine guns would seek to threaten American warships the size of cities on the sea? It doesn't make any kind of sense especially in light of the video release of the Iranian version of the same incident. I bet the Pentagon was shocked to see that Iran also had video of the very same incident but with differing result.

"In a bid to counter earlier Pentagon accusations that the Iranians warned they could blow up the US vessels, Iran's English-language Press-TV broadcast a video showing an Iranian commander in a speedboat contacting an American sailor via radio, asking him to identify the US vessels and state their purpose:"

"Coalition warship number 73, this is an Iranian patrol," the Iranian commander is heard to say in English, asking for the vessel to confirm its number. "This is coalition warship number 73. I am operating in international waters," replied the American voice. State-run Press-TV said the footage had been released by the Revolutionary Guards, the ideological force involved in the incident. The tape showed "warship number 73" -- the USS Port Royal -- looming in the foreground and also showed the two other US vessels in the incident, the USS Hopper and the USS Ingraham. "Request your present course and speed!" said an Iranian commander. For Iran, the release of the footage was seen as buttressing its claims that the incident was purely a routine matter of identification that ended without any disturbance.

Gareth Porter in an interview with Amy Goodman of Democracy Now said, "So I think that the major thing to really keep in mind about this is that it was blown up into a semi-crisis by the Pentagon and that the media followed along very supinely. And I must say this is perhaps the worst - the most egregious case of sensationalist journalism in the service of the interests of the Pentagon, the Bush administration that I have seen so far."

What's even more interesting is that the Pentagon released version of the incident may have been doctored with voice audio spliced over the video which would mean of course that the entire incident was a public relations hoax to garner public support for an invasion of Iran. Americans do not realize that the Pentagon and the Bush administration are continually fabricating and exaggerating video news releases and terror alerts to scare the people into supporting illegal and immoral wars against innocent and sovereign nations.

We must wake up to exactly what is taking place to understand how war is a racket as stated by Major General Smedley Butler way back in 1935. Dwight Eisenhower warned us about the military-industrial complex. John F. Kennedy warned us about secret societies. Now it is up to us to warn each other about how government utilizes and instigates fake incidents to create public support for wars paid for by American taxpayer dollars. Learn your history people; those that do not know it are doomed to repeat it.

> **"As nightfall does not come at once, neither does oppression. In both instances there is a twilight where everything remains seemingly unchanged. And it is in such twilight that we all must be aware of change in the air--however slight--lest we become unwitting victims of the darkness." - Justice William O. Douglas**

-David Dees

The False Left Right Paradigm Continues...
July 2, 2008
Zen Garcia

On November 1, of 2006 I released an article through the Populist Party called Kissing Cousins Staged Elections and the False Left Right Paradigm. In this article I talked about how American politics as well as global politics is nothing more than theatrics, a staged event done for the people's benefit to make us believe we have ultimate influence in the democratic processes of the nations wherein we reside. Politics power and capital have been centralized and controlled by elite who refer to themselves as the Bildeberg Group. This group is well represented by the royal blood line elite, industry philanthropists, corporate moguls, and especially political representatives, who use their domineering position to control, manipulate, steer, and direct the ultimate fate of the world. This global elite group is united by blood, wealth, and bond, oath to unite the planet under global rule or world government.

They desire a global war on terror but want to end national sovereignty and national borders hence the dilemma in America with our borders wide open. In that article I stated, " Now I will make you aware of how phony the left-right, Democratic-Republican, 2 party system which has dominated American politics for 200 hundred years is. 'The so-called Left-Right political spectrum is our creation. In fact, it is accurately reflects our careful, artificial polarization of the population on phony issues that prevents the issue of our power from arising in their minds... We control the Right-Left conflict such that both forms of liberty are suppressed to the degree we require. Our own liberty rests not on legal or 'moral' rights," but on our own control of the government bureaucracy and courts which apply the complex, subjective regulations we dupe the public into supporting for our benefit.' - The Occult Technology of Power

To prove the point I just made, take into account the 2004 election between Kerry and Bush. Do you know that Bush and Kerry are cousins of Hugh Hefner. Ancestry.com revealed also that Bush and Kerry are not only related to Prince Charles, but have a common ancestor, Vlad the Impaler, the real Count Dracula. With that in mind is it even slightly odd that both had sworn blood oaths of loyalty to secret societies (Yale Skull & Bones) which have the destruction of America's national sovereignty for a New World Order one world government controlled by a United Nations Peace Keeping force as their driving motivation. Is it any wonder looking back now that Kerry came out and conceded to his cousin Bush just to stop the recount in Ohio even though he would have easily won the race.

The secret society which owns the allegiance of Bush and Kerry, also owns the allegiance of many of the nation's most powerful men and families. Skull and Bones secretly "taps" fifteen juniors each year, by seniors to head the next year's group. The family names of Skull & Bones roll off the tongue like an elite party list - Lord, Whitney, Taft, Jay, Bundy, Harriman, Weyerhaeuser, Pinchot, Rockefeller, Goodyear, Sloane, Stimson, Phelps, Perkins, Pillsbury, Kellogg, Vanderbilt, Bush, Lovett and on. For a roster of Skull and Bones members

Bruce and Kristine Harrison, Hawaii-based publishers of historical databases traced back the family histories of Bush and Democratic Sen. John Kerry. They found out Kerry and Bush are exactly 16th cousins, three times removed. Playboy founder Hugh Hefner is the president's ninth cousin, twice removed. Both the president and the Massachusetts Senator can claim ties to figures ranging from Charlemagne to Walt Disney to Marilyn Monroe, Harrison said. In his book, "Bush Kerry and Their Other Cousins," Alexander Books explores his own family tree to show how George W. Bush, John Kerry, Dick Cheney, and Senator Johnny "John" Reid Edwards are all related to most of the Presidents of the United States. Think this is the first time cousins have run against each other for the Presidency? Just as in 2004, the elites hijacked the elections in 2000 and had Gore concede the Presidency to his royal cousin George 'the decider' Bush. 2004 was a repeat of 2000 except that it was a different cousin conceding to Bush.

I can't tell you how many e-mails I received after the release of this article calling me whacked and crazy beyond delusional, which at times I may be; but at least I do the research, no matter how strange or insane the truth seemed to be. Sometimes truth is stranger than fiction and unless you do the research how can one tell? Do I think Barrack Obama can restore the reputation that George W. Bush so totally obliterated for this country? No, I don't believe we can right all the wrong inflicted upon the world through this rogue administration. I pray every day for chance for retribution but have no faith in the Washington establishment.

Perhaps he will bring a new direction and resurrect interest especially in young people to be involved in the political process. Having skyrocketed politics in a meteoric fashion, perhaps Barack is a little less tainted by the power elite and the sultry game of buying political favor through corporate lobbyists. Yet is it not strange he too is related to both George Bush and Dick Cheney. Is he just another show pony in the grand theatrics of American politics? I liken the political race to that of the Kentucky Derby in that all of the players are controlled by the very wealthy and very powerful. And though the people come out to participate and take entertainment in the entire event, the truth is they can only hedged their bets on favorites. The favorites themselves are controlled by the money that can afford to finance their political life training and evolution.

Obama, the Senator from Illinois is a distant cousin of George W Bush and 11th cousin of Dick Cheney. The Chicago Sun-Times revealed the genealogical link claiming that they both shared ancestors, Mareen and Susannah Duvall, 17th century immigrants from France. The Duvalls are Obama's great-great-great-great-great-great-great-great-great-grandparents, and Cheney's great-great-great-great-great-great-great-great-great-grandparents, the paper said. George W. Bush and Obama, are 10th cousins once removed - linked through a 17th century Massachusetts couple, Samuel Hinckley and Sarah Soole, according to the Sun-Times. He is also distant cousins of Brad Pitt and direct distant relatives of pres. Gerald Ford, pres. Lyndon Johnson, pres. Harry Truman, and pres. James Madison. He is also a distant cousin of Winston Churchhill and Civil War General Robert E Lee.

Can we trust Obama? I know we can't trust John McCain and Hillary Clinton who are also both tied to the blue blooded elites. Hillary is a distant cousin to Angelina Jolie, singers Madonna, Celine Dion and Alanis Morissette, and is related Camilla Parker-Bowles, wife of Prince Charles in England. John McCain is sixth cousin to First Lady Laura Bush.

34 presidents have direct familial relations and are bound by blood, what does that tell you about the dominance by certain families on the sphere of American politics. "This information comes from Burke's Peerage, which is the Bible of aristocratic genealogy, based in London. Every presidential election in America, since and including George Washington in 1789 to Bill Clinton, has been won by the candidate with the most British and French royal genes. Of the 42 presidents to Clinton, 33 have been related to two people: Alfred the Great, King of England, and Charlemagne, the most famous monarch of France. So it goes on: 19 of them are related to England's Edward III, who has 2000 blood connections to Prince Charles. The same goes with the banking families in America. George Bush and Barbara Bush are from the same bloodline - the Pierce bloodline, which changed its name from Percy, when it crossed the Atlantic. Percy is one of the aristocratic families of Britain, to this day. They were involved in the Gunpowder Plot to blow up Parliament at the time of Guy Fawkes" -Researcher/Author David Icke, "Alice in Wonderland and the World Trade Center"

Did you know all 43 U.S. presidents have carried European royal bloodlines into office? 34 have been genetic descendants from just one person, Charlemagne, the brutal eighth century King of the Franks. 19 of them directly descended from King Edward III of England. Every presidential election in America, since and including

George Washington in 1789 to Bill Clinton, has been won by the candidate with the most British and French royal genes. Of the 42 presidents to Clinton, 33 have been related to two people: Alfred the Great, King of England, and Charlemagne, the most famous monarch of France. 19 of them are related to England's Edward III, who has 2000 blood connections to Prince Charles.

I know Hillary Clinton and John McCain definitely are bought and paid for and will bring us only more of a what the Bush- Clinton dynasty wants, world government through the United Nations, endless and perpetual war in all parts of the world, and protection for Israel at all costs to everybody else even ourselves. I would like to believe that Barack will really bring some positive change and perhaps end the descent into chaos and destruction of the American Republic. I hope he does what he says he will in his very eloquent and moving speeches. I believe in our Constitution and Bill of Rights and will only support those officials and organizations which will defend our liberties and freedoms against terrorists foreign but especially domestic.

I find it very hard to believe in Barack when it is well-known that Zbieginiev Zbrinski is one of his senior current foreign-policy advisers. Zbrinski, masterminded the Balkanization and takeover of not only the oil-rich regions of the Middle East but the movement into Central Asia. It was his grand vision as outlined in his book, "The Grand Chessboard" that initiated Americans current foreign-policy and the shift into preemption and the strategic placing of permanent military bases throughout every region to secure American control of richly laden oil producing nations.

"'World events since the attacks of September 11, 2001 have not only been predicted, but also planned, orchestrated and - as their architects would like to believe - controlled. The current Central Asian war is not a response to terrorism, nor is it a reaction to Islamic fundamentalism. It is in fact, in the words of one of the most powerful men on the planet, the beginning of a final conflict before total world domination by the United States leads to the dissolution of all national governments. This, says Council on Foreign Relations (CFR) member and former Carter National Security Advisor, Zbigniew Brzezinski, will lead to nation states being incorporated into a new world order, controlled solely by economic interests as dictated by banks, corporations and ruling elites concerned with the maintenance (by manipulation and war) of their power. As a means of intimidation for the unenlightened reader who happens upon this frightening plan - the plan of the CFR - Brzezinski offers the alternative of a world in chaos unless the U.S. controls the planet by whatever means are necessary and likely to succeed." - Michael C. Ruppert

I have to doubt that things will really change when the same advisers that led us into the fracas of the war in Yugoslavia, Iraq, and Afghanistan, are still driving the neocon position of preemptive war and global expansion as outlined by the Project for the New American Century's "Rebuilding America's Defenses." I feel Bush will attempt to stoke the war against Iran, Venezuela, and even Pakistan? Who can really tell where the next front is. All I know is that we as a nation as a people as a republic cannot take much more and are running out of time to right the ship. We've arrived at the breaking point. Our soldiers have had it and have been long pushed beyond the courageous limits of duty, honor, and family. They have endured more than they should ever have had to endure as indicative of the epidemic suicide rate among returning veterans. We ask our soldiers to sacrifice for our country but when will our country sacrifice for them? Something's going to give, something's going to break, something is going to snap, what that is I don't know but I do know it can't go on like this very much longer. You can't wage a war, lower taxes for the rich, and borrow money endlessly without something eventually collapsing. America is in so much debt that we are spending 25% of our total GDP just to pay down interest on the debt which increases every moment of every day. It's just a matter of nations cutting off our collateral and abruptly ending the Fed's insane borrowing and marathon printing of the dollar. Once the world realizes that the dollar is worth about as much as Monopoly money, it's over for America.

"No free man shall ever be de-barred the use of arms. The strongest reason for the people to retain their right to keep and bear arms is as a last resort to protect themselves against tyranny in government." Thomas Jefferson

-David Dees

Where are the New Revolutionaries?
July 14, 2008
Zen Garcia

Recently, the U.S. celebrated the birth of its independence. It was on that day that our forefathers declared separation from the tyrannical rule and authoritative oppression so commonly exhibited by the rulers of the British Empire. Such tactics as torture, rape and murder in the most brutal and heinous forms were disguised as municipal law and imposed as legal edicts throughout the empire. Those who dared to revolt against the iron hand of the monarchy were quickly disposed of, held indefinitely, and/or quickly disappeared. Dissent in any form is intolerable. Justice was and is for those who can and could afford it. Brutality was largely expected from those who lived in fear under the bastion of that cruel system of control. Systems of government were long ago seized by the criminal elite and utilized to oppress rather than liberate.

"Give me control of a nation's money and I care not who makes the laws." - Mayer Amschel Rothschild

The mainstream press also has and is largely owned by the elite; was and is used to mislead, misinform and purposely deceive. The press was never used to enlighten or educate- but to manipulate and betray.

Truth is for those who work outside the system. Unwelcomed in mainstream media, it has been and always will be utilized to control, scare, and steer the ultimate fate of the sheeple; who know not that they are imprisoned by their own vain entertainments and mostly meaningless endeavors. The people do not even know that they are being prepared for slaughter.

The ultimate goal of the elite is to decimate the population into the perfect size to serve as a slave class. With the use of vaccines, manufactured disease, depleted uranium, chemtrails, genetically modified food, poisoning of the food and water supply, war, and now with the ultimate evil of unfettered cloning taken place, they are largely succeeding.

Where are the new patriots, the modern day Patrick Henry, Paul Revere, Thomas Paine, Thomas Jefferson, George Washington, and the Marquis De Lafayette? Our country is in need of a revolution. I call on you patriots, rise now in defense of your mother. Rise for your children, and for their children. This nation is in need of heroes. We need those willing to put their energy into action.

If we do not make a stand and make the criminals pay for their misdeeds and have justice served, the rest of the world will have no other recourse than to prepare themselves to battle the greatest evil on the planet as they did pre-Hitler, the danger of the world's strongest nation in the hands of a criminally insane blood thirsty elite. We must rise to safeguard this dream of freedom and those values which we celebrate on this awesome day of our mighty God blessed independence.

How can we the people of this once great nation, a once great people ourselves allow the likes of two really stupid men like George Bush and Dick Cheney, destroy our nation's morals, values, and freedoms and all for the sake of criminal gain? How can we allow government terrorists to control the might, wealth, fate, destiny, and direction of a country which represented to the world that shining jewel of equality; a nation which once preserved government for the benefit of the common good? How could each of us as citizens and benefactors of the legacies of this nation become so complacent as to be totally unaware of the world changing and people impacting decisions being made recklessly by the Washington establishment and Neo-Con hawks bent on a third global war and a renewed crusade.

How can our civilian and military leaders respect or legitimize the authority of the Bush-Cheney administration when it has been so widely revealed that they have committed innumerable treasonous crimes for which they should have long been hung from the gallows?

Hell, that would be too easy for them- I say inject them both with the mercury anthrax vaccines required of all military personnel, and then force feed them depleted uranium so they know firsthand what they've put our soldiers through implementing their foreign policy and yet only the Lord can judge.

I find it difficult to believe that they are still free men- and what shocks me even more is that they remain yet in power. Even after allowing our country to be attacked on 9/11, and forcing the entire military and national defense establishment to stand down, the military still follows order knowing Bush Cheney are still hell-bent on war with Iran. America, do you not understand that we are at the end of our history and that the empire is crumbling around us even now?

Do you not see that our currency is more like monopoly money than any other foreign currency which holds real value? Do you not know that the Amero is already printed and in the banks? Literally, the manure is about to hit the fan, and splatter all over us and yet, we continue as if all is hunkey dorey.

As long as the soap operas, comedy shows, and sports events are still available for viewing, you will sit idly by happy in your blissful ignorance, entertained yet for one more evening. Will you turn off the TV!

Seek out some real news and find out what's really going on - so that we can do something about it. Or, will you ignore the great challenges of today and tomorrow so that those who consider us nothing more than worthless eaters can continue to implement their planetary police state system of oppression and control?

If this is the fate that you want for your kids, and their kids - then surely continue to watch meaningless, non sensible, B.S. tv.- or, like many others now - do your homework - face the facts, get over your fear and come to realization that it is up to us, the true lovers and patriots of this nation to rise up to take on the tyrants who think they are above the law.

Russert: "What does that tell us?"

Kerry: "Not much, because it's a secret,"

Russert: "Is there a secret handshake? Is there a secret code?"

Kerry: "I wish there were something secret I could manifest there."

-Meet The Press, August 2003

Russert: You were both in Skull and Bones, the secret society.

President Bush: It's so secret we can't talk about it.

Russert: What does that mean for America? The conspiracy theorists are going to go wild.

President Bush: I'm sure they are. I don't know. I haven't seen the (unintel) yet. (Laughs)

Russert: Number 322.

-Meet The Press, February 2004

-David Dees

The Betrayal That Lead To The War of Terror
August 11, 2008
Zen Garcia

A few weeks ago a trial took place in Washington D.C. where retired military & active duty soldiers came together as veterans against war to testify about the evils that the military rules of engagement required they commit. They painted stories of horror upon horror inflicted upon the Iraqi people and how our occupation of their homeland justified the raising of an insurgency. They said that nobody could allow themselves to be subject to the treatment that the Iraqi people had been and are still forced to endure/suffer daily because of the occupation. Insurgency is a consequence of occupation, as it would be in any nation among any people across the globe mistreated as the Iraqi nation has and had been. Besides, they remember America supported Saddam Hussein. The majority of the public in Iraq knows this and has requested of their national government an immediate troop withdrawal and yet it does not matter. Why" Because America is an Imperial Tyrant bent on preemptive wars of aggression to seize lands rich in natural resources. The Neo-Con PNAC boys have hijacked foreign policy since at least the creation of the National Energy Policy Development Group, chaired by Vice President Dick Cheney.

The group, commonly referred to as the "Cheney Energy Task Force," produced a National Energy Policy report in May 2001 which detailed Iraqi oil production and reserves. In July 2001 Judicial Watch filed a FOIA request and lawsuit against the administration citing grounds that it was not "in compliance with the Federal Advisory Commission Act (FACA), which mandates that certain documents, task force members, meetings, and decision-making activities be open to the public." Judicial Watch, verified that documents turned over by the Commerce Department, under court order as a result of Judicial Watch's Freedom of Information Act (FOIA) lawsuit concerning the activities of the Cheney Energy Task Force, contain a map of Iraqi oilfields, pipelines, refineries and terminals, as well as 2 charts detailing Iraqi oil and gas projects, and "Foreign Suitors for Iraqi Oilfield Contracts."

Why are madmen allowed to rule the world" I guess it's true what Edmund Burke said, "All that is necessary for the triumph of evil is that good men do nothing." How did we as a world populace ever get so complacent as to let a little man like George W. Bush, "the cowboy decider", destroy the dream, reputation, standing, & stature of a nation rich with history of extending opportunity to all people everywhere; whom values for self and their children, the right of freedom, equality, liberty, justice, and the rule of law. Our forefathers carefully laid out such a beautiful document as the US Constitution and our Bill of Rights to serve as tools to preserve our Republic and yet every day our civil liberties are eroded more and more. Constitutional protections are being shredded by the very lawmakers who swear on the Bible to uphold these sacred edicts.

Thank God at least the United States Supreme Court has been showing some backbone in upholding the Constitution rights of American citizens to own a gun and habeas corpus rights to detainees held as yet indefinitely by the Bush administrations grand sweep of 'enemy combatants' post 9/11. If the Guantanamo detainees are so dangerous that our government found it necessary to torture them for information, then let it come out in a court of law how much they are a danger to our national defense. I feel without question that most of the enemy combatants locked up and awaiting prosecution under a military tribunal are without question innocent of 9/11- as the events occurred that day.

How many of them made the American military stand down as Dick Cheney did - as outlined by Norman Mineta's testimony to Lee Hamilton of the 9/11 Commission claims that Vice President Dick Cheney was in the PEOC (Presidential Emergency Operations Center) bunker when he arrived at approximately 9:25 a.m. the morning of 9/11. Mineta challenged the 9/11 Commission Report assertion that Cheney had not arrived there until 9:58-- after the Pentagon had been hit. Mineta contradicted the commissions account and also revealed that Lynn Cheney, too, was in the PEOC bunker with Condoleeza Rice at the time of his arrival.

"During the time that the airplane was coming into the Pentagon, there was a young man who would come in and say to the Vice President. the plane is 50 miles out. the plane is 30 miles out..and when it got down to the plane is 10 miles out, the young man also said to the vice president "do the orders still stand"" And the Vice President turned and whipped his neck around and said "Of course the orders still stand, have you heard anything to the contrary!"

It must've been a tragic realization for our military men and women in uniform to realize that they had been duped into joining the military at a time when they thought they were going to fight against 'terrorists' whom attacked this country the morning of September 11, 2001. What does one do when life drops a ton of bricks on you, realization alters that which one thought was unshakable reality, and all that one believed they were fighting for becomes meaningless" Many in the world have come to realize that 9/11 was an inside job, Iraq was a target of the Bush White House prior to 9/11, and that some rouge element within the administration has been leading us insanely down the path of global chaos because of collusion between the oligarchy and the fascists political representatives powerful enough and willingly corrupt enough to sell their political will.

How did Dick Cheney force a military stand-down the morning of 9/11 when our military generals had always held the authority, to order shoot to kill directives without consultation should they deem it necessary" The Bush administration introduced a change into the chain of command altering orders which had been established to allow for immediate response to hijack situation. Conveniently altered only months prior to the events of September 11, 2001, issued on June 1, 2001, the document entitle Chairman of the Joint Chiefs Of Staff initiative 3610.01 - An Aircraft Piracy (Hijacking) and Destruction of Derelict Airborne Objects Directive, replaced existing standing orders for dealing with the shooting down of errant or hijacked aircraft, and forced the permission of either the President, Vice President or Secretary of Defense before defensive measures could be implemented. This document lead to Dick Cheney's traitorous forceful stand down of the entire North American Aero Defense establishment insuring a successful 'terrorist' attack followed by 3 large scale controlled implosions the morning of 9/11. This event became the precursor and cause for the invasion and occupation of both Afghanistan and Iraq.

"At a bare minimum, this confirmation by Norman Mineta is in gross contradiction to the 9/11 Commission Report and poses serious questions about the Vice President's role in ordering NORAD to stand down on 9/11. Mineta confirmed his statements with reporters, saying 'When I overheard something about 'the orders still stand' and so, what I thought of was that they had already made the decision to shoot something down.' Norman Mineta made it clear to reporters-- who verified his quotes in written text alongside him-- that Mineta was indeed talking about a stand down order not to shoot down hijacked aircraft headed for the Pentagon. After no shoot down took place, it became clear that Cheney intended to keep NORAD fighter jets from responding-- evidence that Cheney is guilty of treason, not negligence for allowing the Pentagon to be hit." - Aaron Dykes

I would have to see evidence to believe that any of the terrorists housed at Guantanamo and other rendition facilities ever had anything to do with the stand-down of the American military or setting the explosives inside World Trade Center buildings 1, 2, or 7, I doubt whether or not they had any real connections to the real 'terrorists' inside our own government. We may never know because of the nature and secrecy surrounding the military tribunal system. We do know from Able Danger that the real terrorists were protected and enabled and that the Taliban and Al-Qaeda networks were created by the CIA and protected as an intelligence asset. The real criminals are the political liaisons who only act as if they are willing and ready to serve the public interest, but in actuality are wolves in sheep's clothing.

The Bildeberg elite want nothing less than global war as outlined by Albert Pike and the Scottish Rite Freemasonic order. I pray that George Bush does not find or create the opportunity to strike Iran before leaving office. He recently said in interview "I'm not over yet." Pray that nothing like 9/11 happens before the next election cycle. How I wish that we could unite behind an independent candidate. If we could all just trust that a third party candidate could win, and that if we worked hard enough, we could make it happen - what a beautiful change it would be for world!

"We are grateful to the Washington Post, The New York Times, Time Magazine and other great publications whose directors have attended our meetings and respected their promises of discretion for almost forty years. It would have been impossible for us to develop our plan for the world if we had been subjected to the lights of publicity during those years. But, the world is now more sophisticated and prepared to march towards a world government. The supranational sovereignty of an intellectual elite and world bankers is surely preferable to the national auto-determination practiced in past centuries."
David Rockefeller, Baden-Baden, Germany 1991

-David Dees

Subterfuge for Larger Attack on Iran?
August 19, 2008
Zen Garcia

Contrary to mainstream news reports and Western media attempts to finger Russia as the recent culprit for the 8-8-8 Georgian War, European news and foreign press carry quite a different scenario than the one being propagandized here in the United States. CNN, Fox, as well as other syndicates are all reporting domestically that Russia bombed villages before forcefully invading Georgia with the intention of occupying and annexing that sovereign nation. However the alternative press reports that US Special Forces along with Israeli special advisers took part in the assault of Georgian troops into South Ossetia. Bodies of American and Israeli mercenaries were found among the dead. Reports also include the use of highly sophisticated nonlethal technologies to control and disperse civilian crowds.

Why the Georgian military would launch a surprise bombing campaign upon the citizens of those breakaway regions? Reports are that civilians were brutally murdered including women and children. More than 2000 citizens may have lost their lives during initial assault. Russian UN peacekeeping troops tasked with protecting the population of South Ossetia and who had a legal UN mandate to be there, responded in defense as combat erupted on both sides.

Shortly after the initial onslaught, Russia sent military and civilian convoys in to bring aid the people of that region. Western media reports that Russia is in actuality invading and occupying Georgia with intent to either annex or cause regime change. In truth Russian soldiers were sent in to protect citizens of those breakaway regions.

Here's an excerpt from a recent article:

"Russia has moved tanks and troops into South Ossetia to protect its nationals and peacekeepers hours after Georgia launched a full-scale military offensive against its breakaway territory. Russian President Dmitry Medvedev condemned Georgia's attack as an act of "aggression" and vowed to defend Russian citizens in South Ossetia. An overwhelming majority of the region's 70,000-strong population holds Russian passports. "I must protect the life and dignity of Russian citizens wherever they are," said Mr. Medvedev in televised remarks at an emergency meeting of Russia's Security Council on Friday. "We will not allow their deaths to go unpunished. Those responsible will receive a deserved punishment." The Russian Defense Ministry said it was sending reinforcements to Russian peacekeepers in South Ossetia. Ten peacekeepers were killed and another 30 wounded when Georgian artillery and tanks fired point blank at peacekeepers' headquarters and observation posts, said a spokesman for the Defense Ministry. He said Georgian troops were finishing off wounded peacekeepers.'

My question - why attack South Ossetia and why now? Was this a diversion for something else? Are we witness again to that seemingly familiar dance of controlled manipulation to get something else? Did the United States plan on luring Russia into a regional conflict in hopes that they would annex Georgia, occupying their focus for a possible attack on Iran? Did the United States military instruct Georgian military forces to press into South Ossetia as a way to justify a Russian military response? Did the Georgian President believe that NATO would back up his claims to those breakaway regions? Did the US military play him for the fool and betray him and the Georgian nation so that they could move on plans to bomb Iran?

Putin's greatest anger towards Bush, these reports continue, was his foreknowledge that the invasion of South Ossetia by Western led forces was a subterfuge maneuver designed in an attempt to cover the Americans true objective, a limited nuclear strike upon Iran's nuclear facilities, and of which the US War Leader had already given the order to strike. Putin's rapid response to these machinations, however, led to his swiftly contacting the top leadership of the United States Military Command whereupon they swiftly ?crushed' their own President's war plans and removed from the American Nuclear Weapons Chain of Command the US Naval Officer who conspired with Bush to plunge our World into Total War.

"The commander of a Navy air reconnaissance squadron that provides the president and the defense secretary the airborne ability to command the nation's nuclear weapons has been relieved of duty, the Navy said Tuesday. Cmdr. Shawn Bentley was relieved of duty Monday by the Navy for loss of confidence in his ability to command, only three months after taking the job." American Military Commanders then informed Israel that the US would not assist them in their plans to attack Iran according to an article written by Sorcha Faal, entitled, "US Millitary Crushes Bush Planned Nuclear Attack On Iran."

"Israeli government spokespersons Wednesday declined to comment that the American administration has rejected an Israeli request for military equipment and support to attack Iran's nuclear facilities, local daily Ha'aretz reported. The report said that the Americans viewed the request, which was transmitted (and rejected) at the highest level, as a sign that Israel is in the advanced stages of preparation to attack Iran. They therefore warned Israel against attacking, saying such a strike would undermine American interest."

Georgian President; Mikheil Saakashvili announced a future New World Order and attacked South Ossetia at a time when both sides were preparing to share dialogue to find a solution to the two sides differences. Saakashvili announced prior to the invasion on live televised address, "I beg you (South Ossetians) to cease fire immediately. We have no wish to wage war against you. Don't try the patience of our country. Let's stop this escalation and start talks - direct, multilateral, any kind of talks."

This scenario is similar to Saddam Hussein's invasion of Kuwait, in that prior to the invasion he asked what the US government response would be to his annexing Kuwait. He was told that the United States held no interest in that country and that essentially nothing would happen, that there would be no response. However as soon as he invaded Kuwait the United States started organizing a coalition of willing forces to depose of his regime. As a puppet of the United States government he too was duped and betrayed much like Manuel Noriega in Panama.

Is the conflagration between nations about to explode? The pieces on the chessboard are being shifted once again and seemingly every time at the expense of the people of the world who suffer the consequences of those decisions made by unforeseen power brokers representing the criminal elite.

"We shall have World Government, whether or not we like it. The only question is whether World Government will be achieved by conquest or consent." James Paul Warburg, son of Paul Warburg, United World Federalists for a World Government, stated before the U.S. Senate, February 17, 1950.

"By the end of this decade [by the year 2000] we will live under the first One World Government that has ever existed in the society of nations ... a government with the absolute authority to decide the basic issues of human survival. One world government is inevitable." Pope John Paul II as quoted by Malachi Martin, The Keys To This Blood.

"We are on the verge of global transformation. All we need is the right major crises and the nation will accept the New World Order." David Rockefeller.

-David Dees

Remembering the Fallen of 9-11
September 12, 2008
Zen Garcia

A year ago, I released an article at the Populist Party of America entitled, "Open Martial Law Coming to America". In that article I speculated that flight 93, the one shot down over Shanksville, Penn. was headed not for WTC 7 as reported on by Barry Chamish, but for the US capital. I speculated that 9/11 was much like the Reichstad fire, and that like Hitler those forces that pulled off the events of that day seven years ago had originally intended on decimating the US Capitol just as the German parliament had been torched disrupting government function.

Remember it was soon after that Hitler absolved their authority and then pass the enabling act to give him all power to seize dictatorial control of the German state. the same thing happened on the morning of 9/11, the shadow government had already been called into a deep underground bunker and granted authority to take over the active duties of government should something have happened to either the members of Congress or their place of lawmaking.

A quote from that article, "During the Zaccarias Moussaoi trial America was informed by one of the supposed hypothetical masterminds behind the attacks of September 11th, 2001, that Flight 93 had originally been intended to hit Congress. "In the final minutes of Flight 93, passengers attempted to retake the plane at which point the hijackers crashed it into the western Pennsylvania field. The plane had been headed for the U.S. Capitol, according to Sept. 11 mastermind Khalid Shaikh Mohammed." Take this testimony into account with the fact that already in place, was a plan signed by Congress to give dictatorial power to the executive branches of government, meaning the president in times of uncertainty where martial law must be declared; would assume dictatorial powers.

This scenario would have definitely occurred if the Capitol had been hit and the majority of members killed. Why do I believe martial law was the intended consequence for the United States post September 11th? Two sources released a little discussed story of how one hundred of the Republican leaders from all branches of government had already been moved to a bunker and were prepared to take over duties as the official government from that bunker. No Democrat or Independent was invited or even notified including the Minority leadership. It was not until the story was reported by the press that the Democrats learned of the existence of this shadow government.

Should the attacks on America been fully successful, America would already be under open "martial law" rather than the covert one we now find ourselves in. Can you imagine if an airliner dove into the Congress and devastated that seat of government? The Neo-Con Hawks would then have had no problem continuing America unimpeded down the road of imperialistic empire expansion as called for by the Project for a New American Century call for global domination. "

I speculated years ago that flight 93 was originally intended to strike the US Capitol, to destroy that symbol and seed of government invested with the authority and power to balance out the executive branch of government. On the morning of 9/11/01, had the US Capitol been hit, the "shadow government" which was established to protect the continuity of government ensuring continued leadership in times of national crisis, would have lawfully seized control of government and most certainly would have then established and implemented full martial law and a successful coup of the American representative form of government.

The Vice-president, certain members of his staff, along with other Republican Party leaders were quickly whisked to the safety of deep underground bunkers and assigned the task of running government. The Hamadam case further confirmed my suspicions that the US Capitol was the target of flight 93. When the prosecutor delivered his opening statement in the military commission trial of Salim Hamdan - Osama bin Laden's former driver - he said he would show that Hamdan heard bin Laden describe the target of United Flight 93, the hijacked plane that crashed in a field just outside of Shanksville, Pennsylvania, killing all 44 people aboard. Lt. Cmdr. Timothy Stone said bin Laden had said the plane was headed for "the dome," apparently in reference to the U.S. Capitol.

It sickens me that the Bush administration and our government representatives exploit 9/11 as the reason for the war on terror when we know that the real criminals have not been held to account for the murder of thousands of American citizens and that the real criminals are in the halls of government driving a policy of never ending war. Even the patsies blamed by government for the hijacking of those airliners used in the attacks of that day, Al Qaeda and namely bin Laden have also not been held to account. It was July 3 of 2006 that the top CIA group tasked with the capture of Osama bin Laden was disbanded even after the president promised to capture him "dead or alive."

Let's honor those Americans which died on this fateful day seven years ago by waking up the American people to the truth of that day and it's consequence for the war on terror. If those blamed by government for the terrorist attacks of September 11, 2001 are not guilty of the crimes alleged, then who are the real criminals? This is the question that must be answered at all costs especially when our nation is fighting wars on several fronts based on the incidence of that day.

We know that seven of the 19 hijackers blamed for the attacks of that day by the FBI and CIA are still alive and walking free having never been questioned in an American criminal Court. Let's lay the ghost to rest and give them justice for the real crimes committed on that day namely the controlled demolitions World Trade Center 1,2, and 7, not to mention the criminal stand-down of the American military by the vice president Dick Cheney.

God bless all of the families and individuals that lost loved ones or were touched by the grief, tragedy, sorrow of carrying and recalling the painful memories associated to that day. Though I did not lose personally anybody that I knew myself, I share in your sorrow and I feel your pain. I have cried with you. As an American I am empathic to your need for justice, I just question what that justice should be and who it should be focused upon.

We are to protect our nation from threats both foreign and domestic.

"We live in a dirty and dangerous world. There are some things the general public does not need to know and shouldn't. I believe democracy flourishes when the government can take legitimate steps to keep its secrets, and when the press can decide whether to print what it knows."
-- Katherine Graham, Washington Post publisher and Bilderberger

"In the next century, nations as we know it will be obsolete; all states will recognize a single, global authority. National sovereignty wasn't such a great idea after all."
Strobe Talbot, President Clinton's Deputy Secretary of State, as quoted in Time, July 20th, 1992.

Acknowledgements:

Always first and full honor worship praise to the Most High, Creator of the Universe, Father in Heaven, Yahweh, who is all was and will ever be the sum total of all things, the totality of being, His only begotten Son, Yahushuah Savior Messiah, the Word of Yahweh and light of the universe, whom brought creation into visibility and reflection, and to the Holy Spirit in whom all things are dreamt into possibility and birthed into manifest being.

For our every chance to be witness to another moment of grand happening, may we Lord extend ourselves in duty and service to Your people and Your cause, realizing there is no better focus in life worthy of our undivided attention than salvation and eternal life with You. Thank you Yahushuah Savior Messiah for dying on the cross for each and every one of us even those whom deny you, for purging the sins of this evil world and for exampling to us a peaceful and more beautiful way.

To those truth seekers that have dedicated themselves to wearing the full armor of Yahweh and that have stood themselves up sheathing the sword of the Word for battle in this devilishly evil world, whom instead of seeking kingship and authority seek after wisdom and the priesthood rather wanting to serve than glory in self pleasure and seducing glories; always remember the seeker of lost paradise may seem a fool to one who has never sought the other world. – Jim Morrison

To my mother and father, Manuel Pedro and Myong Hwa Garcia, I could not have been blessed with better parents and for that I give thanks to the Creator for the lives we were able to share with one another in this strangest of worlds. I am indebted to you both for life and opportunity, for being the most courageous examples of love duty, devotion, and family that a child could ever experience.

Mom know that I miss you more than I have ever missed anyone or anything and that I pray for your comfort joy peace and serenity every day of my life and that I cannot wait to be with you again where I can just hold you and embrace you once more. Thank you

Lord that my dad is still with me and that we are looking out for one another in best way that we can. I love you both so much, words can never convey the incredible nature of it.

To my son, Justin James Garcia - I honor you my soul twin for opening yourself to the possibilities of relating and for allowing a father with innumerable shortcomings the blessings of knowing you and for blessing me with the incredible experience of simply watching you grow to manhood. I love you so much and am so proud of you. Spirit will be strong with you if you allow it.

To your mother, Stacy Painter Yates, how can I ever exclaim how deeply heartfelt my love is for you, the relating we share through parental connection, and bond we hold through our son. How I wish that all other parents could share such a relating as we. I pray often for your blessing, that of your business, and family.

To my friends, family, extended family, the girls who work for me, I love and thank each of you for your commitment to aiding my independence and lifestyle. Without you it would not even be possible for me to follow my path and serve the Lord. Thank you for your relationships with me, I pray daily that you are everyday blessed in awareness and discernment so that you can see the wisdom of making wise choices in attracting the realities and people that you would want to relate with in everyday life.

To my co-host Alan Swanson, to the www.FallenAngels.TV Community, I thank you all for believing in and encouraging mywork. Much of what I do would not be possible without you. To my colleagues, Dr. Joye Jeffries Pugh, William Kennedy, and to all the others I have been blessed to work with or interview, thank you for sharing with us your lifework and the wisdom that you've been lead to. We don't all agree on everything but that's okay, we can agree to disagree as we have all covered different areas of research. May the Lord continue to bless us in discerning the constantly veiled underlying truth of all things.

Special mention and thanks to David Dees and Toni Christiano: David for allowing me to utilize his incredibly deep with thought, truth provoking images, and graphic designs. It's amazing how your work paralleled the articles that I had written in the evolution of my own Awakening to the New World Order. David's wakening was similarly woven into and throughout his own political commentary and opinion, and while we come from two very different worlds we share a moment of time and history that unifies our work in an effort to awaken others to the New World Order and their unholy agenda. I cannot thank David enough for his kindness in allowing me the use of his work, most artists of his stature and experience would demand a small fortune I would never be able to afford as a humble but comfortably poor servant of the Lord. May Yahweh and Yahushuah take account of your courtesy and reward you justly. Toni, thank you so much for volunteering your time and effort to proofread Awaken and for supporting my work in a way unequalled until now. I thank Yahweh for true friends like you, my family in Christ who help me even to this day. You have made the quick availability of this work possible for the masses.

To my cats, Pretty Princess Fiona and So Handsome Samson, I love you babies so much it is such a pleasure to watch you interact with life in your pure state of joy. I promise, promise to not work so much and to dedicate more time in just being with you but alas you'd have me not work at all and right now that's not possible. I Love You All. May the Lord guide and bless us in those days which are coming upon this unsuspecting world.

Yahweh Yahushuah Bless
Zen Garcia
4:21 pm December 9th, 2010

- The Babies